Accessorizing the Bride

Vintage Wedding Finery through the Decades

Norma Shephard

Schiffer Publishing Ltd

4880 Lower Valley Road, Atglen, PA 19310 USA

392.54
SH

Dedication

For Ardra Leah
and
Norma Corinne

Library of Congress Cataloging-in-Publication Data

Shephard, Norma.
   Accessorizing the bride : vintage wedding finery through the decades / by Norma Shephard.
         p. cm.
   ISBN 0-7643-2185-4 (hardcover)
1. Wedding costumes—United States—History.
2. Marriage customs and rites—United States—History.
I. Title.
   GT1753.U6S44 2005
   392.5'4'0973—dc22

2004031043

ISBN: 0-7643-2185-4
Printed in China
1 2 3 4

Published by Schiffer Publishing Ltd.
4880 Lower Valley Road
Atglen, PA 19310
Phone: (610) 593-1777; Fax: (610) 593-2002
E-mail: Info@schifferbooks.com

For the largest selection of fine reference books on this and related subjects, please visit our web site at
www.schifferbooks.com
We are always looking for people to write books on new and related subjects. If you have an idea for a book please contact us at the above address.

This book may be purchased from the publisher.
Include $3.95 for shipping.
Please try your bookstore first.
You may write for a free catalog.

In Europe, Schiffer books are distributed by
Bushwood Books
6 Marksbury Ave.
Kew Gardens
Surrey TW9 4JF England
Phone: 44 (0) 20 8392-8585; Fax: 44 (0) 20 8392-9876
E-mail: info@bushwoodbooks.co.uk
Free postage in the U.K., Europe; air mail at cost.

Contents

Acknowledgments   4

Foreword by Joan Crosbie   5

Introduction: Dressed For a Day Like No Other   6

Chapter One – 1865-1900: The Victorian Bride   22

Chapter Two – 1900-1910: The Edwardian Bride   40

Chapter Three – 1910-1920: The Changing Role of Women   53

Chapter Four – 1920-1930: The Flapper Bride   63

Chapter Five – 1930-1940: The Depression Era   77

Chapter Six – 1940-1950: War and Post War   92

Chapter Seven – 1950-1960: The Barbie Doll Bride   117

Chapter Eight – 1960-1970: The Second Women's Movement   139

Chapter Nine – 1970-1980: That Seventies Wedding   163

Chapter Ten – 1980-1990: The Power Bride   183

Chapter Eleven – 1990-2000: This is the Nineties   194

Chapter Twelve – Brides of the New Millennium   202

Chapter Thirteen – The Life of a Collection   210

Glossary   214

Bibliography   215

Index   216

Acknowledgments

This book would not be possible without the encouragement and assistance of many people. My sincere appreciation goes to Joan Crosbie, Curator of Casa Loma, for inviting the Mobile Millinery Museum to mount its very first wedding exhibit. The enthusiasm expressed by the thousands of international visitors who viewed *A Wedding to Remember* at Toronto's historic castle in 2001, served to advance our efforts in collecting, preserving, and exhibiting an ever greater number of bridal costumes and wedding memorabilia.

My heartfelt gratitude goes to the former brides and their families who have donated their wedding gowns and treasured heirlooms to our archives, as well as those who have allowed us to borrow special pieces for this project. The names of these individuals are presented in the photo captions, alongside the appropriate illustration.

Special thanks to Heather Darch of *Musee Mississquoi,* for the loan of my great grandmother's wedding gown and to Donna Young, Pat Boyle, and Marie Minaker for their enthusiastic and industrious assistance in gathering gowns and wedding stories from across Canada.

I offer my appreciation to the Burlington Writers group *Quick Brown Fox.* Your expertise and sensitivity in critiquing my work is always welcome.

Finally, a great big hug to Ardra and Corinne for your practical assistance and to Mom and Jim who have been supportive in countless tangible and intangible ways while I dropped everything to do this book.

Foreword

A wedding. There are few family events that are welcomed with such joy and excitement. Regardless of culture, a wedding brings friends and family together in celebration with many traditions and customs surrounding the big event. *Vintage Wedding Fashions Through the Decades* provides a comprehensive, yet intimate look at wedding fashions from 1865 to the modern day.

In the mid-19th century, where the majority of the population was rural, the bride wore her "best" dress for her wedding day. The expense of a dress that was overly ornate, white, or that would only be worn once was not practical. By the late 19th century, a white gown had become the color of choice for the middle classes. Frequently, the dress would be altered and dyed after the event so that it could be worn again. Of course, brides from wealthy families had the luxury of wearing a single use white gown.

While bridal fashions have ebbed and flowed throughout the last century, white (and its subtle variations) remains the preferred color for the wedding gown. Perhaps the greatest change has come not from the fashion itself, but in the expectations of the middle class bride. The late 20th and early 21st century bride has increasingly adopted not only the bridal fashions, but also the elaborate wedding day celebrations that were once reserved for the upper classes. Today tens of thousands of dollars are spent on the wedding event itself; invitations, a romantic venue, flowers, music, a banquet. It is also commonplace to spend thousands of dollars on a gown that will be worn only once and then placed into permanent storage.

Recently, Toronto's historic Casa Loma hosted an exhibit of vintage bridal gowns and accessories entitled *A Wedding to Remember*. The owners of the artifacts were thrilled to be able to re-live their family memories again through this exhibit, and the visiting public appeared equally delighted to share in the memories with them. This is why I believe that *Vintage Wedding Finery Through the Decades* is so special. It not only serves as a detailed guide to the evolution of bridal fashion over the last century and a half, but it brings those once loved gowns, and the special memories associated with them, into the spotlight for a second time around.

—Joan E. Crosbie, Curator
Casa Loma

Introduction
Dressed For a Day Like No Other

A grouping of vintage gowns from various eras.

Every bride whose turn it is to search for that perfect wedding gown, owes a debt to her predecessors. While each generation interprets wedding finery in its own way, renewing and redefining what it means to be a bride, the wedding creations of the past are an ever-present inspiration. From the petticoats and parasols associated with Victorian bustle gowns, to the late 1990s bustiers and pashminas, which punctuate the styles of designers like Vera Wang, this study offers a look at the changing image of brides, with an emphasis on the supporting garments and accessories which add the finishing touch to each unique and timeless style.

Factors influencing bridal design range from social issues, such as war and economic depression, to the inspiration provided by famous brides, whose personal approach to fashion is widely emulated. Some pieces reflect classic styles that endure, while others, like the jumpsuit and hot pant ensembles of the seventies, are of a time only. The gowns within these pages are set in historical context, with notations on design, fabrication, provenance (where known), and estimated current value.

Valuation Guide

Prices for vintage wedding gowns and accessories vary widely depending upon age, style, condition, embellishment, and whether one is purchasing the item at a flea market, thrift store, auction, dealer, or resale bridal boutique. Values given in this book are based upon the price a buyer might expect to pay from a vintage clothing dealer, and are estimated, based upon the condition of the piece, as shown in the photograph. Newer gowns have very little resale value to collectors. Such a gown might be sold second-hand to another bride within two to three years of its original purchase, at 50% of the retail price. After that, the value of a contemporary gown usually depreciates to just a few hundred dollars. Older designs of high quality can fetch premium prices particularly when purchased by brides in search of a unique piece.

Dating a Vintage Gown

Collecting vintage wedding gowns is a sort of fashion archaeology – in the midst of a dig it is easy to spot a terrific find, but it can be more difficult to correctly date and identify the discovery. Unlike other vintage fashions, a wedding gown cannot always be categorized to fit the typical style of a particular era, as it is often fanciful, or selected to match a romantic ideal established in childhood. A bride might, for example, beseech her dressmaker to incorporate a favored design element from an earlier period, or adapt a dress to mimic one her mother or grandmother wore. While one can rely somewhat upon the dominant fashions of an age for an understanding of period bridal wear, it is always possible to come across a piece that might seem anachronistic.

Vintage Wedding Finery through the Ages is organized chronologically to showcase bridal styles prevalent c. 1860 to 2005, with authentic examples of dress designs and accoutrements that typify and in some cases defy, the conventions of each fashion era. Where available, period bridesmaid ensembles and trousseaux items are also included. It is a reference for curators and collectors and a guide for the young girl who chooses to wear her grandmother's wedding gown, or the designer, asked to copy a vintage piece for a contemporary bride.

Many brides begin planning their wedding day in early childhood, inspired by dolls such as this one from the early 1950s.

A plastic doll in 1940s bridal costume.

Ostrich-trimmed Edwardian wide-brim hat.
Mobile Millinery Museum Collection. $150-200.

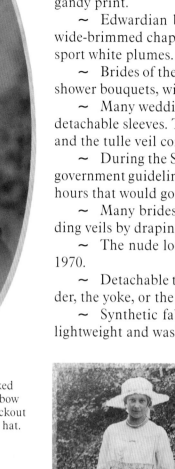

~ Victorian scrapbooks often featured remnants of fabric used to make wedding gowns. These were pasted alongside the names of each bride and the date of her wedding. Many of the fabric swatches were of jewel-toned silk or velvet; some were of linen, cotton, or organdy print.

~ Edwardian brides often topped their wedding gown with a wide-brimmed chapeau. Whatever the color of this hat, it was sure to sport white plumes.

~ Brides of the twenties carried large floral arrangements called shower bouquets, with trailing ribbons and love knots.

~ Many wedding gowns of the 1930s had practical features like detachable sleeves. The gown could later be worn as an evening dress and the tulle veil converted to an elegant stole.

~ During the Second World War, bridal salons had to meet strict government guidelines as to the quantity of fabric and number of man-hours that would go into the making of a bridal design.

~ Many brides of the fifties and sixties made use of their wedding veils by draping them over a baby's bassinet.

~ The nude look was popular with some hippie brides c. 1964-1970.

~ Detachable trains were revived c. 1960 and fell from the shoulder, the yoke, or the waistline.

~ Synthetic fabrics enabled wedding gowns of the 1970s to be lightweight and washable.

Unknown bride c. 1905 in a pin-tucked colored wedding gown. A white satin bow and two wispy white plumes add a knockout punch to her wide-brim astrakhan fur hat.

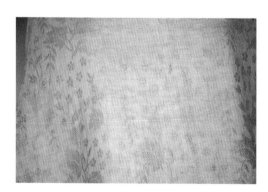

Fabric swatch of white silk jacquard from a Victorian-era wedding gown.

Unknown flapper bride with shower bouquet. Attendants and flower girl also carry large arrangements.

A bridal veils covers a 1950s wicker bassinette, dressed in lace. *Mobile Millinery Museum Collection.* $200-250.

Chapel length satin train attaches with snaps to the shoulders of a matching 1960s wedding gown.

Inez Stansfield accessorizes her 1930s gown with a tulle stole.

When is a gown not a gown?

A wedding gown, loosely defined, is the garment worn by a bride on her wedding day. Whether modest or extravagant, unadorned or ornate, each couture creation, recycled heirloom, or funky improvisation shares a look that is distinctly bridal. There is something about the wedding costume that is special.

For Annie Hudson, it was as simple as the addition of lace trimmings to her cotton, bed-sheet dress, which had been made by a neighbor in 1940. Seamstress Carrie Gregory took time out from raising thirteen children for the project. Several decades later, Judy Pollard accessorized her simple, white, forty-dollar dress with a seventeen-dollar feather boa to create a dramatic bridal statement. Even a best dress, in a color other than white, takes on a bridal quality with the addition of expensive or detailed trimmings.

Bride Judy Pollard accessorized an inexpensive sleeveless white dress with a seventeen-dollar feather boa when she became a bride in 1976.
Courtesy of Judy Pollard Smith.

Ornate wedding point sleeve of a brown silk, knee-length dress, worn by a flapper bride.

For Victorian, Edwardian, depression, and war era brides, a best dress was a practical solution to the question of what to wear on the most important day of a girl's life. An expensive outfit made or purchased for the nuptials, with the expectation that it would be worn on many future special occasions, was a sound economical investment. Only brides from wealthy families could afford a single use white gown.

Jane Hunter chose a skirt and blouse ensemble of blue satin on silk, with a white lace under-blouse, for her wedding to Fred Thomas in 1913. Her older sister, Blanche, was married in a cotton eyelet dress, suitable for social functions following the wedding.

Marriage Advice

Charles Frederick Thomas and Jane Letitia Hunter confirmed their wedding vows by signing their names in a beautifully illustrated marriage certificate booklet, issued to them on July 16, 1913. Inside the booklet were the following instructions to the groom: "The husband must see that the early, tender affection never fails... He must love his wife … down through the declining age to the sunset years, with a love that makes wrinkles beautiful, and infirmities precious."

The bride was reminded that: "The wife and the husband are in a true sense, one. Whatever is good for her is good for him. Let every good wife remember that she is heaven's last best gift to her husband; his angel of mercy; his casket of jewels."

Can a couple live up to such lofty ideals? I believe that my grandparents, Fred and Jane, did. Their home remains for me the brightest spot on earth.

This is a look over our shoulder at those brides who have gone before, a tribute to the skills of their seamstresses and designers, and a sentimental torch, passed to the brides and fashion designers of the future.

Bridal fashion, wedding vows, even marriage itself, has changed a great deal over the years, but one thing remains constant; weddings are about dreams. And for a bride, the dream often begins with a dress.

Jane Hunter chose to wear a dark skirt and a blouse of blue satin on silk atop white lace, for her wedding to Fred Thomas in 1913.

A wedding dress of silk-lined crepe c. 1914, similar in style to Jane Thomas's bridal ensemble. Label: Bourne & Hollingsworth, Oxford St., London. *Mobile Millinery Museum Collection.* $600-800.

Marriage certificate booklet of Mr. and Mrs. Fred Thomas, 1913. *Courtesy of Iris Hillyer.*

Mrs. Blanche O'Brien (nee Hunter), on her wedding day in her "best dress" of white cotton. *Photo by Herbert Simpson, Toronto.*

Elva Barrett gently removes the tulle veil and candlelight-satin Juliet cap from a paper bag in the cedar closet, where her wedding ensemble has been stored for just over fifty years. She points out the tiny beads that have been hand-sewn to the cherished headpiece, then uses one hand to hold the cap to the back of her head and the other to fan the veiling out around her shoulders, as was the fashion when the cap and veil were first worn in 1950.

Elva's satin gown with lace-overlay bodice and peplum, wedding point sleeves, and chapel train required several fittings before its debut so many years ago. The former bride remembers the many bicycle trips she made to the home of her dressmaker, Tilly Weise, often in the pouring rain. Weise also made Barrett's bridesmaids' gowns. The full-length velveteen dresses in rust and green, were worn with matching hand made muffs. Just the thing for an October wedding.

Mobile Millinery Museum Wedding Collection

Elva is one of the many former brides who have contributed to the establishment of the Millinery Museum's Wedding Collection, a segment of which was exhibited at Toronto's historic Casa Loma, in May of 2001. Since that date, selections of vintage wedding costume have toured numerous venues, including a retirement-facility open house in November of 2001. It was a delightful walk down wedding memory lane at the Toronto area residence as seniors scoured trunks, drawers, and closets to produce and display their own treasured wedding keepsakes alongside the costume pieces from the museum.

Young and old, residents and visitors, staff and volunteers, were provoked to smiles and sniffles as they gazed at vintage wedding gowns which had been placed on mannequins throughout the building. Some leaned over stanchions, needing to touch the aged satin, yellowed lace, and delicate veils of long ago. Coordinator, Ann Buczok became so caught up in the day's excitement that she sent home for her own keepsake, which had been cleaned and packed in a box, fifteen years before. Her children gathered round as she broke the seal and removed the lovely lace treasure. She succumbed quickly to cries of "put it on…see if it still fits, let's see how it looks," and modeled her wedding gown for the rest of the day. A neighboring senior read about the event in the paper and rushed over to add her sixty-year-old wedding dress to the collection.

The Mobile Millinery Museum gowns represent the bridal dreams of real women circa 1865 – 2005 and reflect various design elements and fabrication techniques spanning fifteen decades of fashion history. Some gowns come from the fashion houses of New York and Paris, many have been hand-made by a dressmaker or the bride herself, and others were mass-produced and purchased at department stores or bridal salons.

The Bridal Train

While the train was once a fashionable component of ladies wear for day and evening, it is now reserved almost exclusively for bridal attire. It links us with the romantic traditions of the past and is often the most prominent feature of the wedding gown. When viewed from behind during the processional, it has the power to elicit oohs and aahs from teary-eyed witnesses.

Once the ceremony is over, a long trailing skirt becomes impractical. Over the years, designers have conceived several methods of bustling a train or adapting it to be carried. One of the simplest methods was employed during the fifties, when a loop of ribbon, which could be slipped over the bride's wrist, was attached to the hem of the skirt or train. Depending on the type and length of train, this was placed at the end point or even under the dress, several feet up from the hem.

Elva Barrett's beaded headpiece. *Mobile Millinery Museum Collection*. $125-150.

Weightless polyester chiffon train designed to float behind a straight-cut bridal gown c. 1970.

1950s pannier style train or pumpkin skirt, designed to be worn over a sheath style wedding gown. *Mobile Millinery Museum Collection.* $250.

A small, attached train hints at delicacy and femininity while a long sweeping train creates drama. Attached trains are incorporated into the construction of the skirt and can sweep the floor slightly at the bride's heels, form a lengthy extension at the back of the skirt, or broaden the entire hem, forming a pool of fabric that encircles the bride. A detachable train can be fastened at the waist, the yoke (watteau), the shoulders (capelet), or fall from a separate mantle or hood.

Terms like sweep (barely brushes the floor), court (three feet), chapel (four feet), cathedral (six to eight feet), and royal (twelve to twenty feet) all refer to length. Trains are measured at the center back from the waist of the gown to the hem of the trailing fabric. A floor-length adaptation of the train can be worn with a sheath style gown. This can be of the same silhouette as the dress or in the style of an open-front pannier.

Attached cathedral train.

Veils, Hats, Hoods, and Bridal Wreaths

For centuries, ballet costumers have understood the importance of tulle in dressing the feminine form. Layers of this stiff, net material create an illusion of lightness so necessary to a dancer. Likewise, on her wedding day, a woman wishes to look and feel the picture of femininity. At various times in history brides have worn hats, bonnets, floral garlands, or tiaras with their gowns but many feel that a lace, tulle, or chiffon veil is the ultimate crowning touch to a wedding ensemble.

In the Victorian era, veils were not only worn by brides but veiling of different sizes, embellishments, and weights were worn to accessorize day and evening wear. Upper class women wore veiled top hats to formal foxhunts while short, nose-length veils were reserved for their maids and ladies-in-waiting. Colored veils were available for a short period and milliners introduced shaped veils with pink lining at one point but these did not catch on. On the street, swaths of netting were worn as often to attract attention as to escape notice. Transparencies were considered so alluring during the late Victorian era that *What's What* reported "girls who go out alone find a veil a danger rather than a protection, particularly if they be pretty."

By the turn of the twentieth century, specialty veils were designed for travelling and cycling. These could be purchased at a millinery salon or linen draper. With the advent of the automobile, shawl-like scarves or fichus of netting were developed. Tied under the chin, they served double duty; protecting the face from dust and dirt and securing the large motoring hats to the wearer's head.

Victorian women wore patterned net veils, spotted and beaded veils, lace, and mourning veils but bridal veils outsized and out-priced all of these. Traditionally of white or cream colored net, they were a stylish alternative to the white wedding bonnets worn by brides of more modest means. Circa 1900 a bride might spend between two and two thousand dollars for this particular wedding accessory. The customary two-yard-square was usually made of net or white illusion, a transparency that was considered cooler and more becoming than lace. The longer split veil was gathered over cording and secured to the hair so that at the appropriate time it could be opened to curtain the bride and/or act as a train.

Because of their expense, bridal veils were often borrowed. They could become limp. During the mid twentieth century women turned to fashion magazines for tips on stiffening a tired-looking piece. The usual method involved two pieces of waxed paper and a moderately warm iron but women also freshened their veils by dipping them in beer. Previously, they had been stiffened or set in sugar.

Collectors find it easier to obtain early wedding gowns than to secure the matching veils as many of these were loaned out several times during a bride's lifetime and/or passed to subsequent generations. Frail in nature, many were discarded once they became torn or discolored.

Length

Most twentieth century veils are made of net, lace, tulle, or chiffon and vary in size from chin-length to beyond the hem of the train. They may be square, rectangular, oval, or circular, with or without a blusher attachment. They can fall flat over the head (mantilla fashion), or be gathered onto a headpiece, tiara, or hat. A short, layered veil provides balance for a long full skirt, while veiling that trails to the floor or envelops it can soften a narrow, more severe dress.

Many veils have a blusher attachment that is worn over the face for a dramatic entrance. A veil of chiffon or fresh tulle can be bordered with lace, ribbon, or velvet and embellished with chenille dots, lace appliqués, rhinestones, or bows.

Type

~ Flyaway: Usually tightly gathered, it falls to just beyond the shoulders.

~ Fingertip: At least a yard long, the hem of this veil rests at the hip line.

~ Sweep: Designed to complement a dress with a sweep train, this veil extends to approximately one foot beyond the bride's feet.

~ Floor length: Designed to meet the hem of a floor length dress.

~ Court: Will cover a train three feet in length from waist to hem.

~ Chapel: Covers a four-foot train (waist to hem).

~ Cathedral: Up to eight feet long from waist to hem, to swathe a cathedral train.

~ Royal: Up to twenty feet in length from waist to hem of train; seen only in royal weddings.

Underpinnings

In order to show authentic antique bridal wear to its best advantage one must acquire or duplicate the original underpinnings and accoutrements that support and enhance the piece. Imagine a 1950s gown with the post-war extravagance of a multi-layered ruffled skirt, unsupported by one of the crisp tulle crinolines so popular at the time. Or a silk chemise flapper gown without its original satin slip and voluminous shower bouquet. Conversely, try to visualize the sleek lines of a 1930s bias-cut satin gown spoiled by the bumps and ridges of a boned corset. It takes more than a period wedding gown or reproduction dress to create an authentic period look. Foundation garments determine how a dress will hang and what silhouette the body will take.

~ Corsets were needed to achieve the tiny-waisted Victorian silhouette.

~ Wired hoop crinolines, smaller than those introduced ca. 1850 were worn to support the voluminous skirts of the 1860s.

~ Breast suppressors were worn with flapper gowns to create the impression of a flat bust.

~ During the thirties, seamless slips as well as rubber corsets were worn, often without a bra.

~ Strapless, off-the-shoulder gowns and those with illusion necklines required a strapless bra.

~ During the Second World War, slips were often buttoned or snap-fastened as elastic was not readily available.

~ Padded bras or those with demi-cup padding were worn to create the pointed-bust look of the 1950s. Tiered crinolines supported full skirts.

~ The natural look of the seventies was achieved with rounded-cup, soft-style bras.

~ The heavier lace and embroidered bodices of the eighties were worn with a boned corset or long-line bra.

Gloves and Handbags

As a fashion accessory, gloves were once a vital component of every bride's wardrobe. These elegant coverings for the hand endured variations in length from wrist and mid-forearm to elbow, opera length, and beyond. They were constructed of various textiles from leather to lace and adorned at different times with buttons, beading, embroidery, cutwork, and appliqué.

When Annette Marcil wanted the latest in fashionable gloves for her 1940 wedding she cut the fingers from a dotted summer pair, saving herself a modest expense. Bridesmaid Dorothy Simpson remembers wearing "arm coverings in 1946 that ran from the wrist up past the elbow – like a long glove without a hand."

"During and after the war, gloves were as scarce as hen's teeth," one fashion maven recalls but brides continued to make them a part of their wardrobe until the late 1960s.

Reserved in recent years for traffic cops, military parades, and the Royal wave, gloves are once again beckoning to us from shop windows, accessory counters, and bridal processions.

A Progression of Fabrics

Part of the fascination in presenting and viewing a collection of vintage wedding gowns has to do with the number, type, and reason for the various fabrics used in their design over the years. In the Victorian era, wedding gowns were fashioned of natural fabrics comprised of cotton, linen, silk, or wool. Additionally, horsehair, straw, and whalebone may have been incorporated into the construction of the garment or its underpinnings.

Three-tiered bridal crinoline with snap closure c. 1940. *Mobile Millinery Museum collection.* $120-150.

A purse-shaped vase of tulips forms a centerpiece for a spring bridal shower.

These satin fingerless gloves, designed to match a bridesmaid's
gown were known as mitts during the thirties, forties, and fifties.
Mobile Millinery Museum Collection. $35-50.

Gathered silk lace c. 1925.

By 1924, a man-made fabric called rayon was developed, based on cellulose derived from wood pulp. Originally marketed as artificial silk, rayon was not widely used until the 1930s but by the 1950s there were over one hundred different fabric blends with rayon as their primary component.

True synthetic fabrics originated with the development of nylon by the Dupont Company in the late 1920s. Nylon stockings were first offered for sale in 1940 but the Second World War curtailed their availability. Immediately after the war, nylon parachutes were sold to consumers and recycled into wedding gowns and lingerie items. A decade later the sale of nylon-based textiles superseded that of natural fabrics.

By the 1960s dressmaking supply stores offered courses in sewing with the new polyester or bonded fabrics. Since then, the proliferation of synthetic textiles has not let up. In the 1980s, materials like crystalette, a stiff transparent synthetic with a metallic sheen, lent themselves nicely to the creation of fantasy wedding gowns.

Inner view of a 1980s gown made from a bonded fabric.

Cream chantilly overlays a 1960s wedding skirt.

New Life for Old Gowns and Veils

Many a wedding gown has been cut down over the years and fashioned into a party dress or ball gown to be worn throughout the early years of marriage. Wedding dresses and the veils that topped them have also been recycled into special occasion garments for children. In 1894, a bride in Wisconsin made a baptismal dress for her five offspring from the material in her late Victorian wedding gown. Josephine Krismer's creation was handed down through five generations and worn fifty times, over one hundred and ten years.

Old wedding gowns can be put to many new uses, regardless of condition. Seamstresses have reworked wedding dresses into everything from bridal hankies to Halloween costumes. In the 1950s, countless young girls of the Catholic faith took their first communion in an adaptation of their mother's wedding veil, which might have been used earlier to cover a bassinet. 1970s bride, Denise Crockford, used her sewing skills and imagination to transform her wedding gown into a Halloween costume so that her daughter could feel like a princess. Teacher Patricia Boyle offered her once-in-a-lifetime dress to a class of school children for dress-up purposes. More recently, sentimentalists have preserved wedding dress remnants for shadow box displays.

A bride's dual-layered Edwardian wedding dress was remade into this lengthy christening gown. *Mobile Millinery Museum Collection*. $350-450.

The hem has been raised to just below the knee making the former wedding gown suitable for cocktail parties.

A remodeled 1950s wedding gown. *Mobile Millinery Museum Collection.* $200-250.

Chapter One

1865 – 1900
The Victorian Bride

A Montreal bride in a jewel-toned
wedding dress c. 1880.

With the advent of photography came the Victorian custom of posing for a studio portrait in one's wedding finery. Brides in such photos were often attired in elaborate white wedding gowns, following the style set by Queen Victoria in 1840 and sustained by Princesses Vicky and Alice.

In the 1860s, wealthy brides or those of significant social standing were married in white dresses with full gathered skirts and fitted, high-necked bodices. Most of these gowns were not true white, but ecru, dove, ivory, or oyster due to the properties of the fabric used and the bleaching techniques available at the time. The dresses were intricately constructed with multiple, complex fastenings and worn atop corsets with steel ribs or whalebone stays. The bridal attendants were similarly dressed in their own white dresses, supported by crinoline petticoats. With the difficult and time-consuming laundering methods of the day, white dresses were a status symbol as they could not easily kept clean unless one had a staff of servants.

A great number of young women in the mid-Victorian era were married and photographed in colored day dresses, accented with a bonnet or veil. Until the widespread use of aniline and sulfur dyes in the 1870s, these colored dresses were from textiles tinted by vegetable dyes, indigo root, or the cochineal beetle and faded easily. Women were careful to cover the shoulders and bodice of their dresses with complementary wraps, visites, shawls, or sunshades while outdoors.

For formal wedding gowns, the addition of a train and the decision as to its length depended upon a Victorian bride's social status. Socialite brides in Canada who expected to be presented at the British Royal Court would select a wedding gown that might later be adapted for this purpose. A Victorian groom's attire might be blue or wine-colored.

In the 1870s and 1880s white remained the color of choice for moneyed brides but the use of exciting new synthetic dyes, derived from coal tar, made intense colors like claret, amethyst, and deep browns possible and quickly became popular with the middle classes. The original aniline dye, called mauve, was a deep fuchsia, which tended to fade easily to the hue we now associate with that color term.

Victorian brides selected veils or white wedding bonnets to accessorize their gowns as well as wreaths of myrtle or orange blossom. When these were out of season, wax stand-ins were a pretty alternative. Bouquets were in the nosegay or easy-to-hold tussie-mussie style.

Victorian brides were bold with color and arranged flowers more for their significance than for their appearance or fragrance. A bouquet of forget-me-nots, red and white roses, and yellow poppies, for example, would translate to a bridal wish for fidelity unity, and wealth. Dandelions might even be added to the mix to ensure the bride's wishes would come true. Orange blossoms and baby's breath symbolized fertility, and myrtle was worn to ensure devotion. For a bit of extra luck a Victorian bride might have a silver dollar sewn into the hem of her wedding gown.

Second Day and Going-Away Dresses

A Victorian "Second Day" dress could be as expensive and often more elaborate than the wedding gown itself and formed the cornerstone of a wealthy bride's trousseau. After the wedding night, a bride would present herself to friends and family in this decorative colored dress, which would be worn later to other weddings and special occasions.

A practical but attractive travelling ensemble or going-away dress was also a must and would be topped with a carefully selected chapeau. For girls of certain strict religious orders, a going-away ensemble was one opportunity to dress in something a little fancy. Such a bride might be allowed to add a bit of lace and some French ribbon to a brown, black, or green bonnet.

Bridal Hankies

Victorian brides carried lace-trimmed or embroidered bridal hankies, which were stored away with the wedding gown or handed down to sisters, daughters or granddaughters to be tucked into a wedding bouquet years later. These might be monogrammed or decorated in a romantic heart, lovebird, or seasonal motif.

The Wedding Apron

In Victorian Britain, it was church custom that the wedding party fast before the ceremony, necessitating a morning service. A feast or wedding breakfast would be held immediately following the nuptials. As the bride was usually married in her best dress, she protected it at the breakfast with an apron made especially for the occasion. During the 1870s, draped, apron-like panels were sometimes incorporated into the design of the wedding skirt. By the 1880s, British parliament permitted afternoon weddings and many brides on both sides of the Atlantic chose to be married in a going-away dress.

Bride Kate Philip poses for her wedding portrait c. 1895. Her right hand is concealed by a wedding hanky while her left sports a fingerless lace glove.

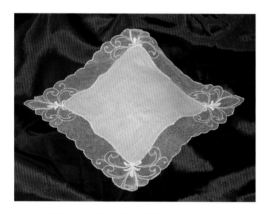

Silk bridal hankie with lace edging, embroidered in a fleur-de-lis motif. *Courtesy of Marie Minaker.* $8-12.

Bridal hankie in concentric squares of lace and cotton voile. *Courtesy of Marie Minaker.* $8-12.

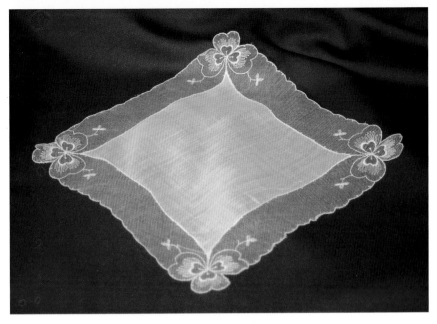

Silk bridal hankie, edged in lace with shamrocks embroidered on each corner. *Courtesy of Marie Minaker.* $8-12.

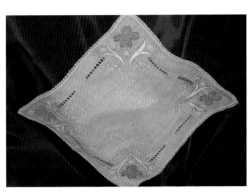

Linen bridal hankie of dove gray cut work. *Courtesy of Marie Minaker.* $8-12.

A dainty hankie of cotton voile for a mother-of-the-bride. *Courtesy of Marie Minaker.* $8-12.

Victorian bridal hankie of silk, edged in lace with raised flowers. *Courtesy of Marie Minaker.* $15-18.

The center of this cotton batiste bridal hankie has been replaced and trimmed in pink, for a bridesmaid. *Courtesy of Marie Minaker.* $8-12.

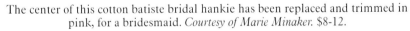

Something blue for the bride to tuck into her bouquet; a finely embroidered bridal hankie of handkerchief linen. *Courtesy of Marie Minaker.* $8-12.

C. 1860: silk and velvet wedding cloak in brilliant red. Ruffles of hand crochet lace trim the collar, sleeves, back, center fronts, and postillions. This surprisingly light-weight wrap was worn to protect the wedding gown from fading. *Mobile Millinery Museum Collection.* $1200-1500.

Sleeve detail matches center front medallion on dress at right.

The original silk tartan wedding gown c. 1860 was cut down and restyled for a 1920s bride. *Mobile Millinery Museum Collection.* $600-800.

The satin lined six-foot detachable train is heavily padded.

C. 1865: This upholstery-weight, ivory duchesse formal wedding gown was made in Quebec by *Glover, Fry & Co, Dress & Mantle Makers*. The boned bodice with hook-and-eye closure sports *Kleinert Dress Shields,* which still contain absorbent charcoal. (These were likely added at a later date when worn by a second bride as Kleinert's was established in 1869.) The satin empiecement is overlaid with ruches of transparent lisse. The waist is wrapped in pleated silk and finished with a trailing bow. A double bow punctuates the corsage. *Mobile Millinery Museum Collection*. $2500.

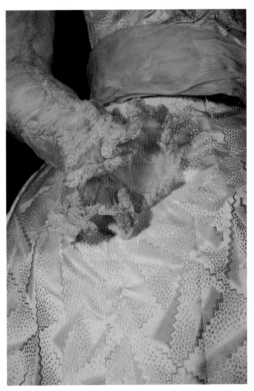

The sleeves, of ruched lisse, are capped with a double ruffle and finished at the wrist with a tapering ruffle to cover the hand.

Inner view of corseted bodice.

The front and side panels of the skirt are shaped without pleats or gathers while the back panel is tightly gathered at the center. The skirt fastens just to the left of a padded envelope pocket constructed to form a bustle. Skirt and detachable chapel train are each lined with a ruffled satin balayeuse.

Label printed on inner waistband of heavy twill.

View showing bustle at center back as well as beading on yoke and sleeve.

Inner view of bodice showing complex hook-and-eye closure.

Tricolor visite has yoke of braided silk threads.

C. 1865: Bride's second day dress of pink and cream striped bengaline with attached sweep train. *Mobile Millinery Museum Collection*. $1500-2000.

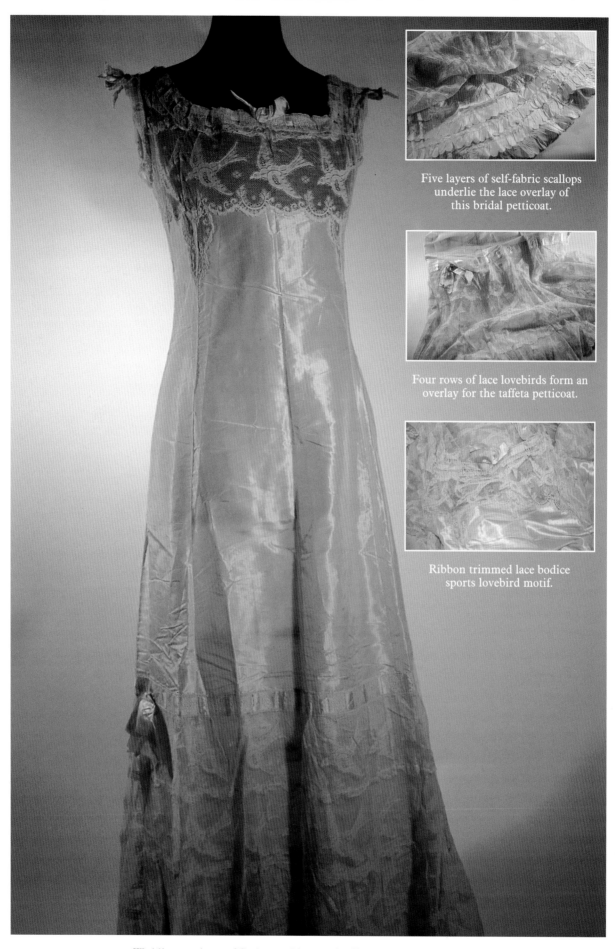

Five layers of self-fabric scallops underlie the lace overlay of this bridal petticoat.

Four rows of lace lovebirds form an overlay for the taffeta petticoat.

Ribbon trimmed lace bodice sports lovebird motif.

Wedding petticoat of flesh-toned lace and taffeta c. 1865. This garment, trimmed with pink satin ribbon, was worn over a corset with both the wedding gown and second day dress. *Mobile Millinery Museum Collection*. $400-500.

This linen capelet was worn by a bride c. 1870 to protect the bodice and shoulders of her wedding gown from fading in the sunlight. Tassels of silk-covered wooden beads hang from ribbon stars at the center front. *Mobile Millinery Museum Collection*. $175-225.

Wedding bodice of dotted silk velvet c. 1860. *Mobile Millinery Museum Collection*. $250.

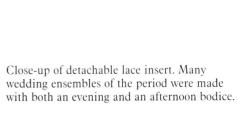

Wedding bodice lined with ladies cloth and supported by nine metal stays. Seams are overcast to prevent fraying.

Close-up of detachable lace insert. Many wedding ensembles of the period were made with both an evening and an afternoon bodice.

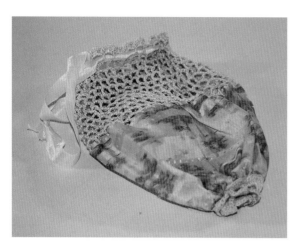

French ribbon of watered silk forms the foundation for this delicate bridal bag. *Mobile Millinery Museum Collection.* $60-75.

C. 1865: A beaded silk bow, trimmed with silver fringe forms a delicate bridal headpiece. *Mobile Millinery Museum Collection.* $30-40.

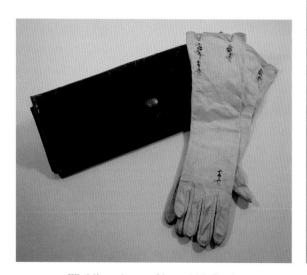

Wedding gloves of ivory kid, finely embroidered in a rose pattern with seed beads for a Victorian bride. *Mobile Millinery Museum Collection.* $125-150. Green leather glove case: $75-100.

Short hoop crinoline of the1860s, often worn over colored petticoats. $250-350.

Back view shows
peplum, double
bands of narrow
velvet ribbon and
silk fringe.

This wedding gown of patterned brown silk, made in one piece, was worn by bride Maria Isabella
Stewart February 14, 1872. Detachable lace collar and cuffs. Buttons appear to have been added
at a later date. Silk has begun to deteriorate in places. *Courtesy of Dianne Wood.* $700-800.

1887 burgundy bustle wedding gown of bride Christina Ferguson. The dress was trimmed in black lace to honor the groom's first wife, who had died in childbirth. Dress is shown with a gold brooch and locket; gifts of the groom. *Courtesy of Musee Mississquoi Museum.* $1000-1200.

Close up of bodice showing bride's gold locket
and pin, gifts from the groom, Alex Philip.

Inner view of bodice showing metal stays.

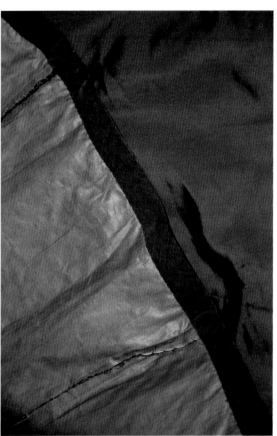

Interior view of Christina Ferguson's
wedding skirt lined with brown ladies
cloth and hemmed in red velvet.

Close up of bride Christina Ferguson's wedding
locket and love letters written to her new husband.

Back view of bodice. Yoke of pleated silk, lace embellishments.

Matching petticoat with flounces of silk taffeta. *Mobile Millinery Museum Collection.* $150-200.

Headpiece of wax orange blossoms and split veil are a nice complement to the gown. Headpiece: $150.

Wedding gown of ecru weighted silk made in two pieces with detachable cummerbund. The weighted silk lining of this gown is literally at risk of going to shreds each time it is handled or exposed to light. The disintegration is a result of harsh chemicals used to enhance the drapeability of the fabric when it was new. The costly silks treated in this fashion became heavier and were sold by weight. Attached sweep train. *Mobile Millinery Museum Collection.* $800-1000.

Unlined drawstring bag. Tulip motif. *Mobile Millinery Museum Collection*. $60-75.

A bride's handbag of crocheted cotton lined with red silk. *Mobile Millinery Museum Collection*. $60-75.

Victorian camisole of cotton eyelet with drawstring waist. *Mobile Millinery Museum Collection*. $60-75.

Cotton drawers with lace flounces falling to just below the knee. *Mobile Millinery Museum Collection.* $125.

Hosiery box of burgundy velvet has silk cover depicting 1860s ladies costume. *Mobile Millinery Museum Collection.* $75-125.

Silk lined hosiery box showing Hanes label.

Cotton camisole edged in pink crochet for a Victorian bride's trousseau. *Mobile Millinery Museum Collection.* $175-250.

A bride's parasol banded in white c. 1870. *Mobile Millinery Museum Collection*. $350-400.

Calico print parasol with wooden handle. Used by a bride c. 1860 to protect the shoulders of her gown from fading. *Mobile Millinery Museum Collection*. $300-350.

Yellow silk parasol bordered with white silk ruffles c. 1900. *Mobile Millinery Museum Collection*.

Chapter Two

1900 – 1910
The Edwardian Bride

A formal bridal gown at the turn of the century usually consisted of a bodice and narrow skirt with self-fabric cummerbund. A wide, beaded neckpiece, which came to be known as a bridal collar, was partially attached to the bodice and could be fastened with hook and eye closures at the center back or pinned with a bar brooch at the front. Informal gowns might be low-cut at the neckline and worn over a chemisette or modesty panel. Fabrics were light, creating a softer look and washable kid gloves rose to meet three-quarter sleeves.

Bridesmaids' gowns were similar in silhouette to those of the bride and followed the current style for afternoon wear; pastel-colored, long-skirted dresses with bodices that pouched at the waist. These were often worn with large hats. By 1907, a one-piece "Princess style" dress appeared.

Corsets remained in fashion, and in major cities, women would shop for these undergarments at specialty shops or corsetieres. Corsets were fashioned with attached garters and usually worn over a cotton shirt and under a cotton or silk corset cover. The Josephine Sykes corsets had the reputation of being uncomfortable but effective. *What's What*, of London, 1902 reports "we would not dream of wearing them ourselves but they are successful in reducing almost any figure to fashionable dimensions." Even children and young girls were corseted and British mothers were advised to consider an American made product for the job, something constructed of "rational stays." These were available only at Evans in London but most North American dress shops had their own in-house corsetiere.

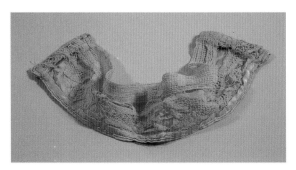

Stand-up collar with metal stay, known as a bridal collar, is a detachable component of an organdie print 1902 wedding gown.

Lace-trimmed modesty panel for an Edwardian wedding gown. *Mobile Millinery Museum Collection.* $75-100.

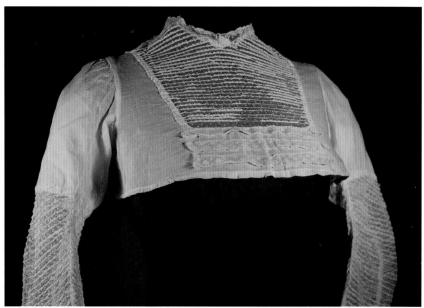

Cotton chemisette with yoke and sleeves of pin-tucked lace, c. 1910. *Mobile Millinery Museum Collection.* $150-200.

On March 31, 2002, Annie Kerfoot Rodgers' two-piece organdie print wedding gown became one hundred years old. The special dress, wrapped in cotton and stored in a box for over a century, was handmade by the bride's sister for an Easter Monday wedding in their family home. A yellowed clipping from the Barrie Examiner Newspaper attests: "the scene within the home of Mr. Joseph D. Rodgers …was in pleasing contrast to the inclement weather outside. There was being performed that day the always interesting ceremony of uniting the hearts and hands of a young couple in the holy bonds of wedlock."

The society reporter goes on to describe the bride as "one of Barrie's fairest maids" and reports that the bride wore a dress of "dainty organdie with point lace trimming" and a going-away gown of brown ladies cloth with matching hat. The bride's sister wore gray organdie. The wedding couple was to honeymoon in Toronto and Prescott.

Some months prior to the March nuptials, a younger sister of the girls had died, prompting the couple to plan a small, quiet celebration but this did not influence the color or design of the wedding gown as the dress had been made the year before.

The first decade of the 20th century is named for Britain's King Edward VII. During this period, scientific advances altered the lifestyles of young women with central heating, plumbing, and electricity entering their homes and making their lives easier. Many of the social imperatives around manner and dress were abandoned as modernists embraced art, entertainment, and conspicuous consumption.

Trends in London shaped North American attitudes to bridal fashion as Canadian socialites were still being presented to the British court, but the salons of Paris continued to hold the prevailing influence. Wealthy new world brides who wanted to be *au courant* with French couture could buy their gowns personally while on trips abroad or select the latest Parisian models from dress shops in major cities. Rural brides and those of more modest means might have a local dressmaker recreate something pictured on a French fashion plate or use their own sewing skills to fashion a special dress.

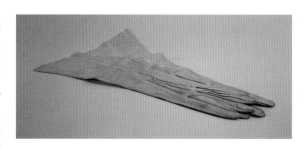

Hand sewn wedding gloves of washable kid with pearl button closure at wrist were made to complement a three-quarter length sleeve. *Mobile Millinery Museum Collection*. $45-55.

Bib shaped modesty panel of exquisite lace. *Mobile Millinery Museum Collection*. $100-150.

Bridal hankie of Annie Kerfoot Rogers in ecru handkerchief linen with point lace trim. *Margaret Lee Collection, Mobile Millinery Museum.* $15-20.

Photo of Annie Rodgers in her wedding gown, which she wore again for her child's christening.

Side view showing pin-
tucked sleeve.

Detachable cummerbund
with metal stays.

Detachable dust ruffle for
inner hem of skirt.

1902. Three-piece organdie print wedding gown, worn by Annie Kerfoot
Rodgers March 31, 1902 is shown with her marriage certificate.
Margaret Lee Collection, Mobile Millinery Museum. $800-1200.

A silk corset cover and creamy white silk stockings from Edna Goddard's wedding day.

Right:
Edna Goddard's wedding corset, fashioned from French ribbon and laced up the back, is shaped by long metal stays. Corset fastens in front with metal hooks and posts. Silk ribbon ties adorn the front garters.

Edna Goddard's "wedding pants."

Edna Goddard's 1905 wedding ensemble has survived complete with two silk petticoats, a satin slip, undershirt, corset with corset cover, silk stockings, pantaloons, veil, and bridesmaid's dress. The gown of tulle overlay was a Paris original and has been lovingly preserved in a cedar box made especially for this purpose by the groom.

Opposite page:
A Paris-original formal wedding gown fashioned of silk tulle with appliquéd lace. Worn by bride Edna Goddard, October 4, 1905 in Lewiston, Maine; worn a second time by Edna Goddard's daughter in 1938. *Mobile Millinery Museum Collection.*

First inset:
Close-up of bodice showing beaded wedding collar, ruffled yoke and sleeve.

Second inset:
Edna Goddard's lace-trimmed bridal hankie.

Third inset:
Edna Goddard's "wedding shirt" of lace trimmed cotton.

One of Edna Goddard's many silk petticoats. This one of cream silk, with sweep train is layered with several narrow flounces at the hem.

Edna Goddard's tulle wedding skirt hangs over a wedding chest which was custom-made by the groom and contains Goddard's three-piece wedding gown, her sister's bridesmaid's dress, two silk petticoats, one satin slip, one pair silk stockings, a corset, corset cover, pantaloons, undershirt, headpiece and veil. *Donna Fochuk Collection, Mobile Millinery Museum.* Trunk and contents: $2000-2500.

Close-up showing wide cummerbund and transparent, three-quarter sleeves.

Lace-trimmed bridesmaid's dress of pink silk with dotted net was worn by Edna Goddard's sister in 1905 and Beryl Doris Goddard in 1938. Silk cummerbund, hook and eye closure at center back.

Parasol of cutwork linen. *Mobile Millinery Museum Collection*. $250-350.

Ecru linen wedding skirt and matching parasol c. 1905. *Mobile Millinery Museum Collection*. Skirt: $200-250.

Ecru blouse of Battenburg lace for a wedding in the parlor, c. 1905. *Mobile Millinery Museum Collection*. $500-650.

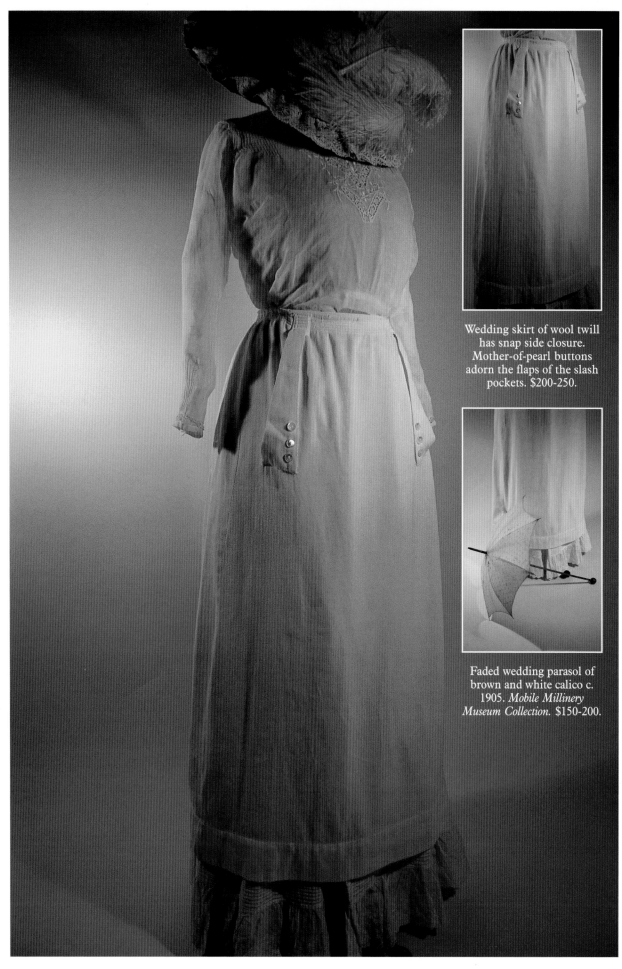

Wedding skirt of wool twill
has snap side closure.
Mother-of-pearl buttons
adorn the flaps of the slash
pockets. $200-250.

Faded wedding parasol of
brown and white calico c.
1905. *Mobile Millinery
Museum Collection.* $150-200.

Informal wedding ensemble for a rural bride c. 1905.

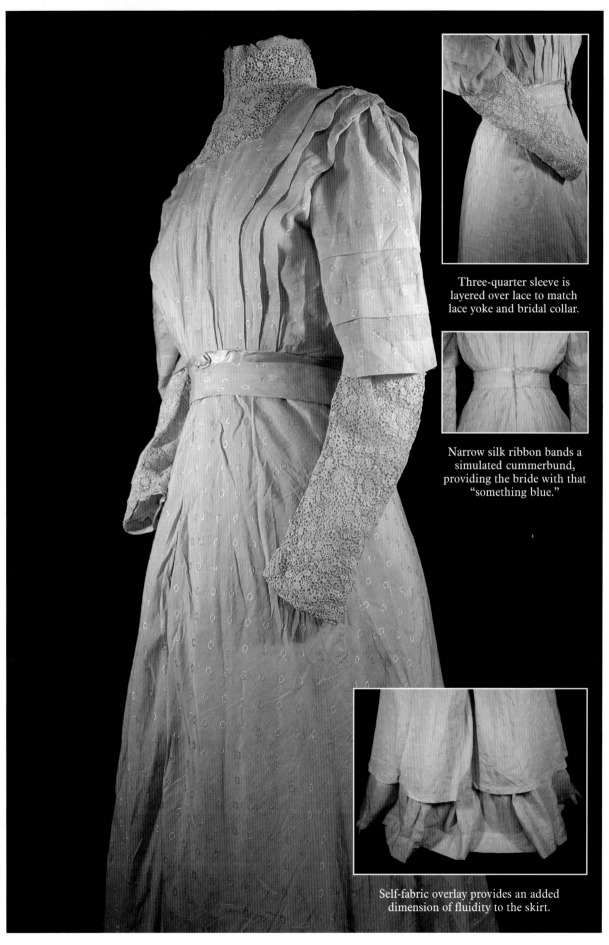

Three-quarter sleeve is layered over lace to match lace yoke and bridal collar.

Narrow silk ribbon bands a simulated cummerbund, providing the bride with that "something blue."

Self-fabric overlay provides an added dimension of fluidity to the skirt.

Winnipeg bride Ethel Tennant was right is style when she chose this one-piece dotted silk gown for her wedding on January 25, 1905. The uncorsetted bodice and limp fabric create a delicate impression in keeping with the new softer look in vogue at the time. *Courtesy of Mary Spencer*. $450-500.

Black lace binds collar and cuffs to match vertical columns at center front.

Edwardian wedding blouse lined with georgette. Cuffs, collar, and midriff boast white crewelwork on blonde net with bodice and upper sleeve of shadow work lace. A dozen fabric covered wooden buttons dot the center front under a bow of spotted black lace. Center back hook and eye closure. *Mobile Millinery Museum Collection*. $500-600.

Black velvet boater trimmed with creamy white ostrich plumes for an Edwardian bride. Crown lined with buckram and black ladies cloth. *Mobile Millinery Museum Collection*. $200-250.

Wedding blouse of ivory silk chiffon over pink satin with horizontal lace insert, c. 1913. Silk covered wooden beads punctuate the sleeves and bodice. *Mobile Millinery Museum Collection*. $600-700.

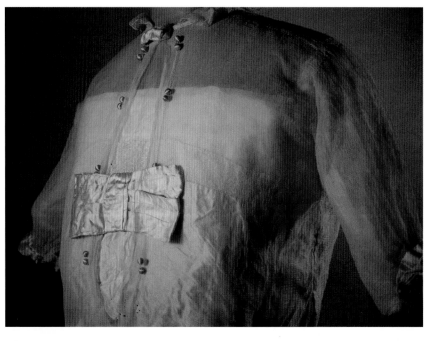

The glass beads, which underlie a layer of silk gauze, capture light when the body moves.

Delphos dress in its twisted state.

This Delphos dress was chosen by an Ontario bride c. 1910. Its flowing lines of finely pleated watermelon silk are preserved by rolling the dress and twisting it into a ball for storage. These dresses were originally sold in small oval hatboxes. *Mobile Millinery Museum Collection*. $8,000-10,000.

Silk streamers weighted
with wooden beads create
center back interest.

Trousseaux gown of silk and rose-patterned gauze has three-quarter sleeve and
pigeon breasted silhouette. *Mobile Millinery Museum Collection.* $800-1000.

Chapter Three

1910-1920
The Changing Role of Women

On July 28, 1913 bride-to-be Jane Christina Philip wrote the following in a love letter to her intended: "I got my dress. I'm sure you will think it's pretty. It's cream serge trimmed with white satin so now if anybody asks you, you know. I went up to see those suits at Goodwin's but they were not nice and anyway none of them fit me. I'm glad they didn't as I think that the dress I got to-night is ever so much nicer and it only cost a few cents more." The following day, Miss Philip's fiancé, Harry Hillyer, wrote back to say "I went downtown yesterday and was measured for a blue suit according to your wishes. I'm going to save enough for a white tie." Jane and Harry were married a short time later but by April 1917 Harry was killed at Vimy Ridge, leaving Jane a widow.

The second decade of the 20th century was one of changing roles for women. With Canada entering the Great War in August of 1914 and the United States following suit some time later, North American women entered the work place in large numbers. During the First World War (1914-1917) women's fashion changed frequently in keeping with the many new roles taken on by the fair sex and wedding costume kept pace with new attitudes.

In 1916, skirts, which had previously rested at ankle length, rose to six inches above the ground. A year later, they rose a further two inches. Fashion influences borrowed from the military appeared, such as epaulettes and sailor collars. Women married in travelling suits atop blouses with large collars. By the end of the decade hems fell once more but colors borrowed from the military (brown, blue, and khaki) remained popular, even for bridal wear.

Wedding photo of Harry Hillyer and his bride Jane Christina Philip on their wedding day in 1913. The bride wears a cream serge dress atop a high-necked chemisette, accessorized by a wide brim hat, white gloves, and shoes. The groom is attired in a blue suit and bowler hat with white shirt and tie. *Photo by Grenier, Montreal. Mobile Millinery Museum Collection.*

Wool traveling suit of the type chosen by some World War I era brides as an informal wedding ensemble. Straight skirt falls to five inches above the ankle. *Mobile Millinery Museum Collection.* $500-600.

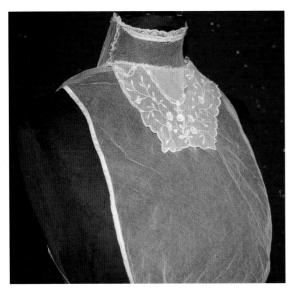

Lace-trimmed cotton chemisette with boned bridal collar. *Mobile Millinery Museum Collection.* $75-100.

Jane's reference to a suit is in keeping with the Edwardian trend amongst working class brides of marching down the aisle in a tailored suit and frilly blouse. Her own gown with its narrow skirt and three quarter sleeve is worn atop a high-collared chemisette and dominated by an extravagant ostrich-trimmed, wide-brim hat. Similar hats were a lovely complement to the draped bodice and hobble skirt effect popular circa 1912-1913.

The outsized hats of the period were also associated with the suffrage movement. Women had been advocating for the vote since 1850, but in the teens they held parades and public demonstrations wearing enormous toppers that came to represent the greater status they sought. Ornamented hatpins, used to secure a hat and its trimmings to a woman's upswept hair, were seen by some to correspond to the fairer sex's new "prickly" nature.

Umbrella-brim straw wedding hat layered with fine lace and white ostrich plumes. *Mobile Millinery Museum Collection.* $225.

Unknown bride c. 1910 in a jewel-toned taffeta suit and lace-trimmed blouse. The wedding hat appears to be of horsehair straw trimmed with white ribbon and fresh flowers.

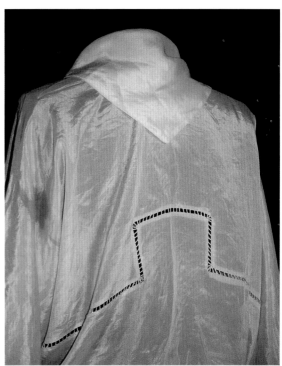

Wedding blouse of pink silk boasts a V-shaped collar, which resembles a scarf when worn over a jacket. *Mobile Millinery Museum Collection*. $250-300.

Rae Hillyer was attired in her best dress and ostrich plumed hat when she married Will Hillyer c. 1914. The groom, who served in the First World War, looked dapper in his uniform.

Gray spats were often worn by grooms at formal and informal weddings. *Mobile Millinery Museum Collection*. $50-75.

Kitty Hillyer's fashionable wedding gown
c. 1912 is worn atop a high-necked, sleeved
chemisette. Her veil is caught up with artificial
flowers to form a helmet-style hat and falls to
the waist atop a trained, hobble skirt. *Mobile
Millinery Museum Collection*.

This pink, trained bridal gown c. 1912 is similar in style to that worn by Kitty
Hillyer. It is of pink chiffon with pleated satin cummerbund and self-fabric
rosette. The draped bodice and sleeves are trimmed with cream lace and
dotted with silver sequins. The pink silk lining is fitted with a three-inch dust
ruffle. *Mobile Millinery Museum Collection*. $1200-1500.

Narrow silk flounces float above a sweep train.

Rural bride Lydia Teel accessorized her two-
piece white cotton wedding gown with a large
fabric hair bow, white gloves, and shoes.

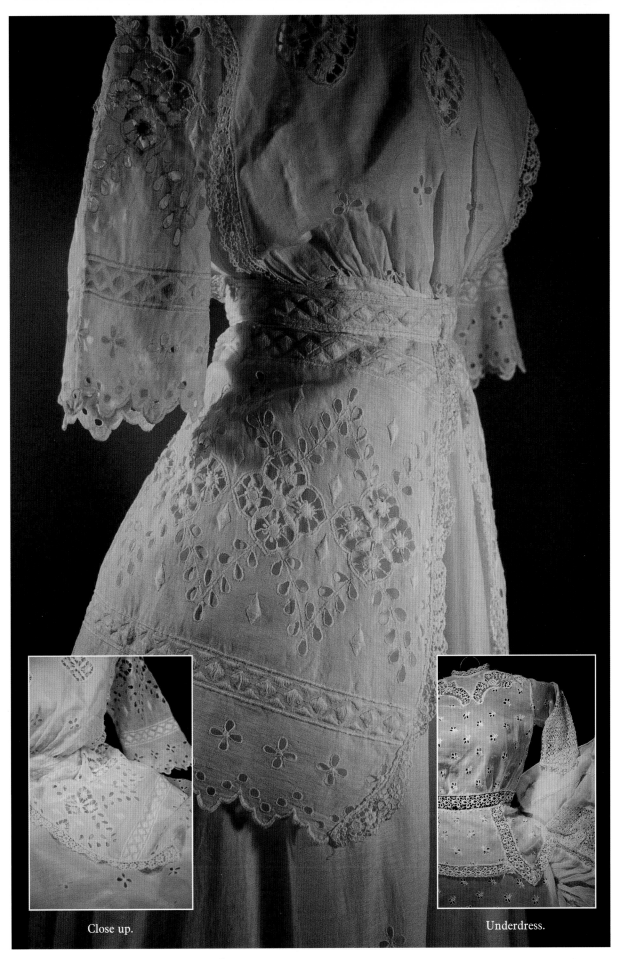

Close up.

Underdress.

This wedding gown of *broderie anglaise* is really two dresses, one
overlying the other. *Mobile Millinery Museum Collection.* $750.

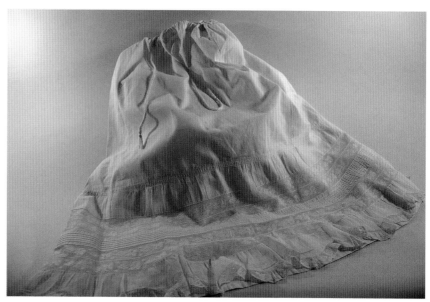

This cotton petticoat was an essential element to the wearability of a cotton eyelet gown. *Mobile Millinery Museum Collection*. $75.

Edwardian veil of silk tulle on a headpiece of wax orange blossoms. $200-250.

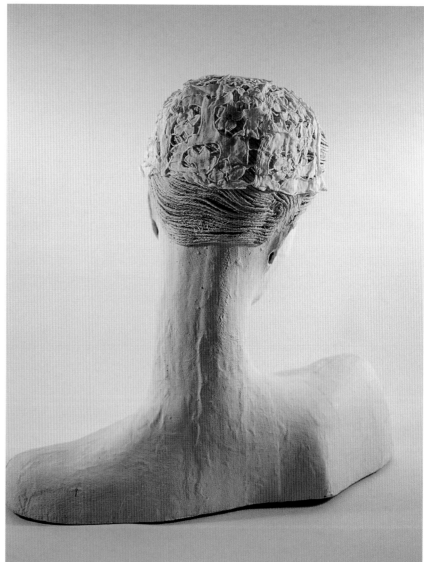

Opposite page:
Muslin wedding gown with hobble skirt c. 1912. A narrow band of cutwork lace joins the pintucked bodice to the gathered skirt. Net-lined skirt is gathered again below the knee to join bands of intricate lace. The lace is repeated on the cuff of each drop sleeve. Worn with washable kid gloves. *Mobile Millinery Museum Collection*. $600-800.

Left inset:
A band of intricate lace covers button closure of back bodice while petals of lace curtain a triangular lace insert to create an ultra feminine look.

Right inset:
Close up.

Juliet cap of cotton eyelet. *Mobile Millinery Museum Collection*. $60-80.

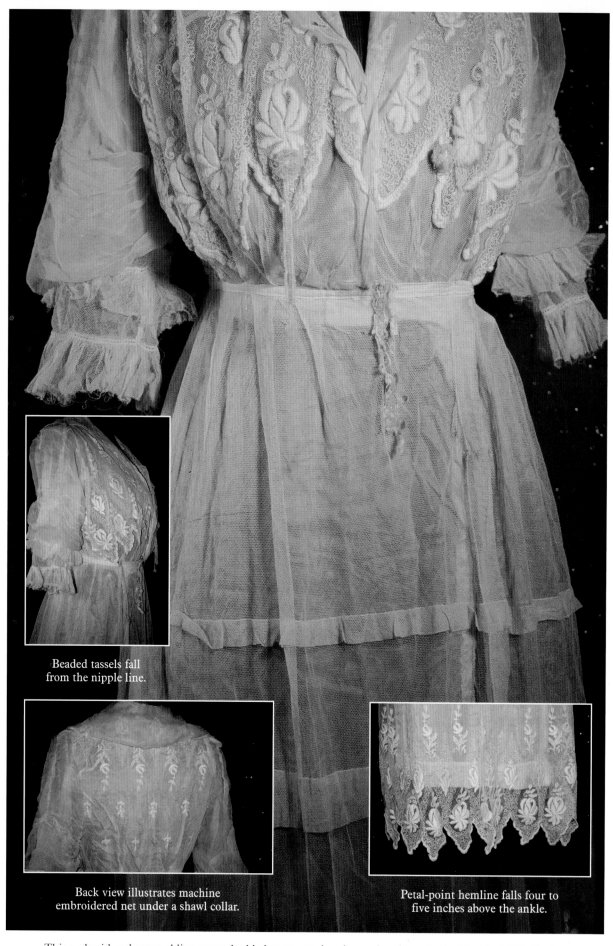

Beaded tassels fall
from the nipple line.

Back view illustrates machine
embroidered net under a shawl collar.

Petal-point hemline falls four to
five inches above the ankle.

This embroidered net wedding gown doubled as an evening dress when it made its debut in 1918. Similar gowns were available for purchase from Canada's Eaton catalogue for approximately $32. Note the beaded tassels, which fall from the nipple line. *Courtesy of Linda Francis.* $450-550.

Attached bolero with center
front, pearl button closure.

View showing re-embroidered lace.

Sash and hem of ivory satin ribbon.

One-piece wedding gown of embroidered lace with double sleeves is lined in silk.
Label: Eaton's, Made in Canada. *Mobile Millinery Museum Collection.* $600-700.

A silk camisole and petticoat c. 1915. *Mobile Millinery Museum Collection.* $125-150.

Veil of ivory georgette worn with gown shown on previous page. Original owner may have removed the satin ribbon bow from her dress to form a headpiece. Lace edging has been added to this veil at a later date. *Mobile Millinery Museum Collection.* $350-450.

This lace-edged net wedding gown with apron panel skirt and three-quarter sleeve was fashioned to be worn atop a similar underdress. *Mobile Millinery Museum Collection.* $350-450.

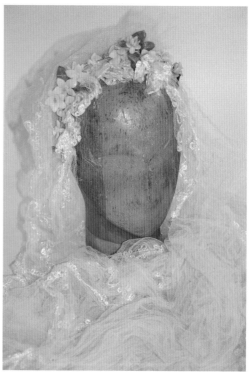

Silk tulle veil with crown of waxed orange blossoms c. 1918. *Mobile Millinery Museum Collection.* $250-300.

Chapter Four

1920 – 1930
The Flapper Bride

Brides of the 1920s had several styles and hem-lengths to choose from. Informal flapper gowns hung sack-like to the knee; formal wedding dresses swept the floor, often with long narrow trains; and semi-formal bridal ensembles fell in handkerchief points at mid-calf. By 1929, bridal hemlines hung lower in the back than in the front, exposing white shoes, decorated with buckles, pearls, or flowers.

Wedding gowns were simply cut, shapeless, and designed to slip on over the head. Dropped waistlines emphasized the hips. Sleeveless gowns were worn with over-the-elbow gloves and generous rectangular cap-veils slipped to the brow line, covered the hair, and enveloped the body. Headpieces were elaborate to complement bobbed locks and

Chicago bride Agnes Lidell in a sleeveless flapper gown, elaborate silk headpiece and embroidered tulle veil.

Orange blossoms dangle from the ribbon streamers of Ella South's bridal bouquet.

might consist of pearls, floral wreaths, or satin braids. Cloche hats, pamelas, and open crowns also made the bridal scene.

By 1926, weddings were performed later and later in the day and knee-length, chiffon dresses with elaborate beading were popular with those brides who wanted their wedding gown to serve as a dance dress following the ceremony. Tube-like shapeless rubber corsets, with garters attached, were worn under these slinky dresses and brides flattened their chests with breast suppressors. It was fashionable, if not necessary, to dress *sans culottes* as the pantaloons of previous decades were bulky and too long for shortened hemlines. Bare arms were popular, strings of beads were worn, and women made up their faces with rouge, eye shadow, and lipstick.

On the heels of World War I, rich browns and striking navies were accepted for a time but white held its position on the bridal fashion stage until 1922 and 1923 when young women caught royal-wedding fever. Britain's Princess Mary and Lady Elizabeth Bowes-Lyon (later the Queen Mother) each wore wedding gowns shot with silver, setting a trend that was copied by many North American brides. The popular magazine, *Harper's Bazaar* also featured a silver gown on its cover in the early 1920s. To complement these dresses, bridal slippers were made of cloth of gold or silver and adorned with marabou, ostrich tips, or shoe buckles of pearl and/or cut steel.

Pastels were highlighted in 1928 when the premier couturier, Molyneaux, designed a wedding dress of yellow georgette with a pink tulle veil for his summer collection. Whatever the color choice for her gown, a flapper bride was likely to carry an enormous shower-bouquet. Many of these cascaded with trailing ribbons, tied into love knots, to hold even more flowers.

The dropped waist of this flapper bride's gown is accented by a corsage of fresh flowers. Maid of honor Mildred Philip wears a deep-crowned, feather-trimmed hat.

Opposite page:
Wedding gown of silver cloth with point sleeves and sweep train c. 1920. *Marie Minaker Collection, Mobile Millinery Museum.* $800-$1000.

Some tarnish is visible on bodice.

Fingertip veil of stiffened net falls
from a cloth-of-silver Juliet cap.

Deatils.

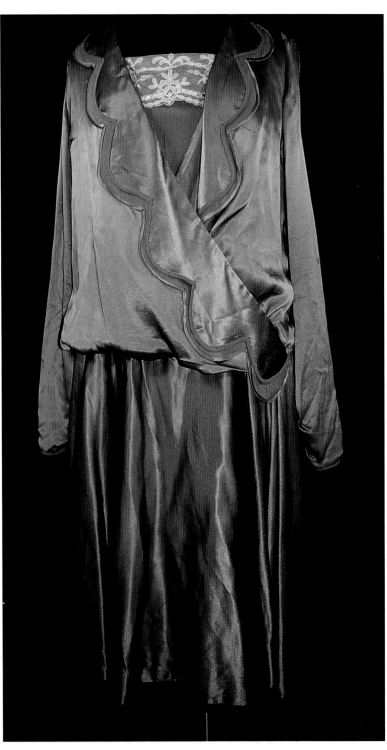

Bride's hat of brown velvet is covered with bronze lace and banded with pink blossoms. $60-80.

Informal flapper gown with wedding point sleeves and pink silk lining has scalloped collar and deep V insert edged with border of ribbon-trimmed lace. *Mobile Millinery Museum Collection*. $350.

A cluster of pearl-dotted self-fabric rosettes conceals a wrap-around construction.

Inner view of drop-waist reveals five fabric-covered weights.

Bertha Aiken married Thomas Rice June 29, 1923 in this champagne gown of lace and silk crepe.
Inner net bodice has hook and eye closure. *Courtesy of Mrs. Rice*. $700-800.

Headpiece of wax orange blossoms, 1921. *Mobile Millinery Museum Collection.* $80-120.

Nine-foot lace mantilla veil with silver ribbon headpiece. *Mobile Millinery Museum Collection.* $450-550.

This crin straw pamela was hand stitched in concentric circles from the center crown for a 1920s bride. *Mobile Millinery Museum Collection*. $50-75.

This wedding gown of lemon yellow silk was purchased in the costume department of *Bourne & Hollingsworth*, Oxford St., London W., c. 1925. The bodice is lined with fine net and decorated with wax orange blossoms. The yoke of dotted net may have matched the bridal veil. *Mobile Millinery Museum Collection*. $800-1000.

Taupe lace flapper gown, lace overdress, and matching hat on wire frame worn by bride Anne Hilton of Ansonia, Connecticut in 1925. *Mobile Millinery Museum Collection.*

View showing irregular hemline.

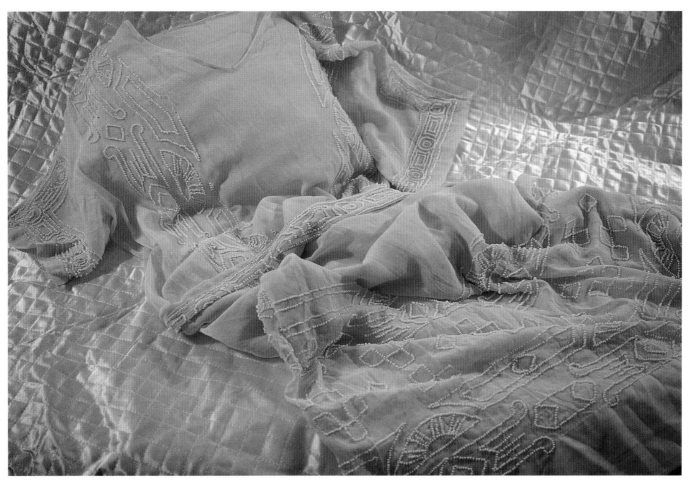

Pastel pink wedding gown of cotton batiste has survived from the 1920s in immaculate condition. Self-fabric belt is attached at the waist and beaded with white seed beads in a geometric pattern to match the dress. Three inch opening at left underarm. *Mobile Millinery Museum Collection.* $800-1000.

There is a hint of pink in this embroidered net veil, which envelops a wire-framed headpiece. *Mobile Millinery Museum Collection.* $150-200.

Close up of hem showing beadwork, which is repeated on the bodice and sleeves.

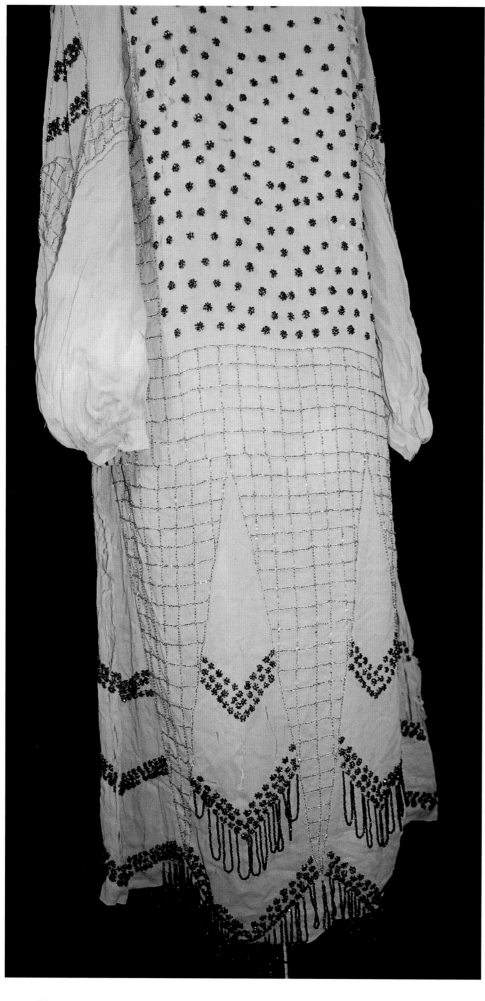

This beaded dance dress of sand georgette is of the type chosen by many 1920s brides. Skirt front shows navy bead clusters and crystal beads in a geometric pattern. Originally worn by Mrs. Daniel Shier. *Maryan Tisdale Collection, Mobile Millinery Museum*. $750.

Detail of beading.

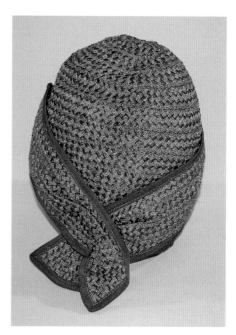

This Wedgwood blue, ribbon weave cloche, handmade for a flapper bride, is lined with silk. Label: Clover Leaf Hat. *Mobile Millinery Museum Collection*. $175-225.

Three lace bands of silver thread create interest on the center skirt panel.

The buckle emphasizes the silver theme.

Cream-colored silk ribbon bow falls from the hip line at the center back.

Underarm snap closure.

This exquisite flapper wedding gown of silk chiffon made a second trip down the aisle for the bride and groom's fiftieth wedding anniversary. *Courtesy of Cathi Gunn.* $1500-1800.

Mantilla veil of white silk is enhanced by a delicate lace border. A bridal bouquet motif of silk thread embroidery at pin-tucked crown is repeated three times. A pair of soft pink bows adds the final touch. *Mobile Millinery Museum Collection*. $250-300.

Many 1920s brides were accessorized in black like the owner of this lace and horsehair pamela hat with celluloid bird. $200-250.

As above.

A bride's horsehair pamela, hand painted in a floral motif. *Mobile Millinery Museum Collection*. $150-200.

A bride's woven straw cloche adorned with brown rooster tail feathers. *Mobile Millinery Museum Collection*. $300-350.

Embroidered silk net veil on a circlet of pearl flowers and gelatine leaves. *Mobile Millinery Museum Collection*. $150-200.

A bride's glistening rhinestone bag. *Mobile Millinery Museum Collection*. $150-200.

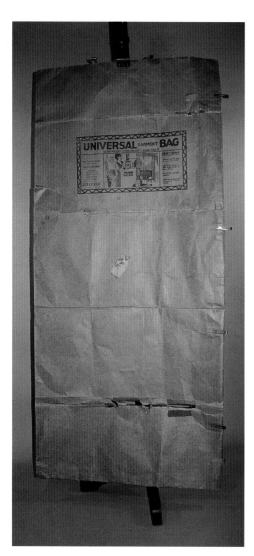

The "Universal Garment Bag" boasts of being mothproof, dust-proof, damp-proof, and airtight.

A cedarized paper garment bag with metal side clips, used for garment storage. *Mobile Millinery Museum Collection.* $75-100.

A flapper bride in a wide brim straw. The ribbons of her shower bouquet trail below the hem of her gown.

Chapter Five

1930–1940
The Depression Era

From 1929 until 1939 the world suffered a severe economic crisis, triggered by the stock market crash of 1929. This period of unemployment, bank failures, and factory closures, now referred to as the Great Depression, created a greater rift between the rich and the poor than there had ever been before. The wealthy and the impoverished alike, however, looked to the cinema for escapism as it was a very affordable means of entertainment.

Hollywood did its best to supply the population with glamorous heroines in luxurious circumstances and sensational costumes. Sensuous fabrics closely outlining the female form lent themselves beautifully to the silver screen and to fashion photography. Gowns, similarly styled to those of the stars, were soon being manufactured for the masses and a brand new wedding look was born.

With the invention of the bias-cut in fashion design, wedding gowns of the thirties took on a slender silhouette. Slinky fabrics were worn close to the body over satin slips or bras and tap pants. Brassieres now came in individual cup sizes providing a better fit. They were usually made of satin and might be ornamented with lace.

Some gowns featured underarm closure and many fastened up the back with as many as forty satin-covered metal buttons. Hairstyles complemented the new sleek profile and veils were attached to simple caps, which hugged the back of the crown over locks of shoulder-length wavy hair which had been permed or curled by means of metal crimping clips.

Detail was reserved for sleeves which, if long, tapered from plump, pleated caps and, if short, achieved fullness with ruches or ruffles. Both joined padded shoulders. Designers helped brides to achieve a look of Hollywood glamour and many young women selected gowns that could also be worn as evening dresses. Luxurious browns, reds, and blues were seen on brides once again.

With economic hardship, many brides had to make their wedding gown serve several purposes. At the outset of the depression, Irene Campbell became Mrs. Grant Adams in a cowl neck, bias-cut gown of black velvet, accessorized with pearls and a marquisette pin. A matching hat dipped stylishly over one eye. The society pages of her local paper headlined "Forsaking Tradition, Bride Wears Black." Her husband remembers her unusual bridal choice as "sensational."

Furs, wraps, jackets, and jewelry added drama and a hint of opulence to colored wedding gowns. Rhinestone pins, hair clips, and bracelets shone against a backdrop of lace, chiffon, crepe, velvet, or heavy satin.

Bride Francis Brewis in an ashes-of-roses satin gown, October 1, 1938.

Irish bride Bridgit Crannay became Mrs. Fergus Philip in a hooded gown of tulle and lace at St. Brendan's church Montreal, September 30, 1935.

Center front gathers end in a self-fabric rose.

Handkerchief hem is punctuated by fabric rose buds.

Pamela style horsehair wedding hat banded with satin-back crepe to match the wedding gown above. *Courtesy of June Gall.* $125.

Sleeveless flapper gown of satin-back crepe, worn by Amelia Jane Carpenter on her wedding day, September 2nd, 1931. Piping separates the bodice from a lace and net overlay skirt. Snap closure at left underarm. *Courtesy of June Gall.* $800-1000.

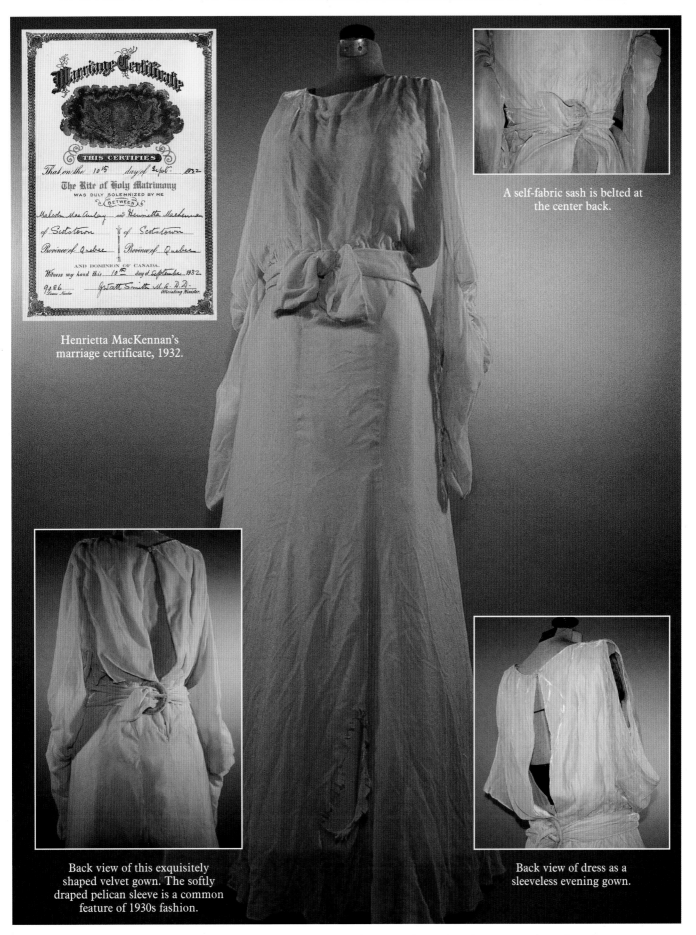

Henrietta MacKennan's
marriage certificate, 1932.

A self-fabric sash is belted at
the center back.

Back view of this exquisitely
shaped velvet gown. The softly
draped pelican sleeve is a common
feature of 1930s fashion.

Back view of dress as a
sleeveless evening gown.

This two-piece silk velvet wedding gown is typical of 1930s styling and can be worn as a long sleeved garment or sleeveless with a matching tulle stole. The cream gown was selected by Henrietta MacKennan for her wedding to Malcolm MacAulay, September 10, 1932 and survived complete with love-knotted, satin ribbon from the bride's bouquet. *Mobile Millinery Museum Collection.* $1200-1500.

Similar wedding gown of apricot velvet with bustle detail at
center back. *Mobile Millinery Museum Collection.* $500-600.

Lace-trimmed hem.

Cream satin wedding gown, comprised of six panels, is shapeless except for subtle gathers at the bust line. Self-fabric sash ties loosely at the back. Neck and hem adorned with lace. *Mobile Millinery Museum Collection*. $450-550.

Cream satin gown shown with reversible cloak of black silk velvet. Cream-on-black printed silk in a falling leaves motif for an autumn bride. *Mobile Millinery Museum Collection*. $600-700.

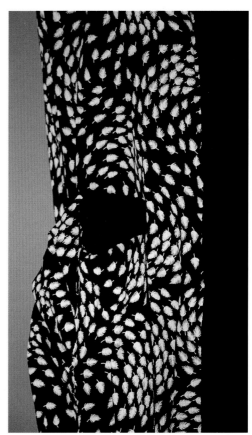

Raglan sleeve, ruched at the elbow.

After its trip down the aisle in the early 1930s, this bias-cut jewel-tone wedding gown of lace and slipper satin served as a ball gown for the new bride. *Mobile Millinery Museum Collection.* $200-300.

View showing sweetheart shaping where lace bodice meets satin gown.

Bias-cut, lace-paneled gown, bolero jacket and underslip of rayon satin, 1934. *Mobile Millinery Museum Collection.* $800-1000.

V-neckline is visible under chiffon bolero.

1930s grape chiffon overlay with self-fabric belt and
rhinestone buckle has gold thread embroidery. $500-600.

Matching bolero jacket of grape chiffon
has short sleeves with ruched hem.

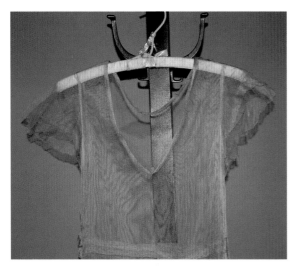

View of the bodice shows deep V
neckline and cap sleeves.

Gored skirt allows for eight multi layer
ruffle inserts.

Wedding gown and bolero cape of turquoise tulle fastens with snaps under the
right arm. Underslip of matching satin has not survived. Worn by Alice Wall Scott
on her wedding day in 1935. *Courtesy of Pauline Paynter.* $300-400.

Opposite page:
Simple gown of eggshell satin with attached
chapel train, has back button closure and
pleated sleeves, ending in a wedding point.
Mobile Millinery Museum Collection. $600-800.

Slipper satin gown with attached cathedral train is pieced from ten panels of fabric to create a fitted bodice and circle skirt. Label: Miriam Originals, New York. *Mobile Millinery Museum Collection*. $1000-1200.

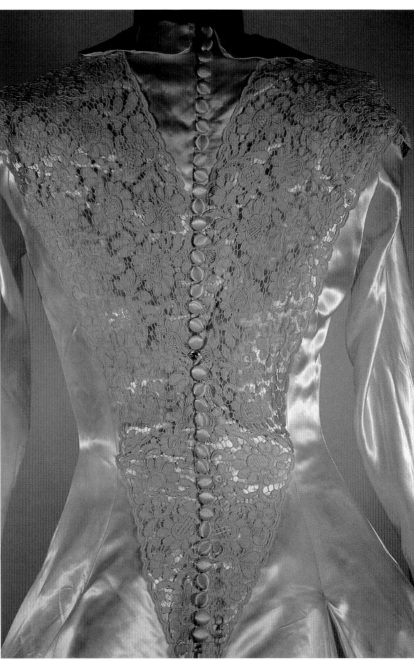

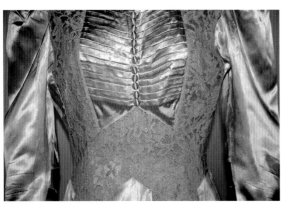

A breastplate of continuous tea-colored lace frames an insert of pleated satin.

Thirty-eight satin-covered buttons extend from neck to tail.

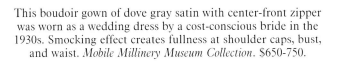

This boudoir gown of dove gray satin with center-front zipper was worn as a wedding dress by a cost-conscious bride in the 1930s. Smocking effect creates fullness at shoulder caps, bust, and waist. *Mobile Millinery Museum Collection.* $650-750.

Top right:
Braided coils of slipper satin at midriff and sweetheart neckline match the bride's braided coif. *Mobile Millinery Museum Collection.* $600-800.

Center right:
Matching gown of slipper satin for a nine-year-old junior bridesmaid. *Mobile Millinery Museum Collection.* $250-300.

Right:
Back view.

Eileen Punnett married in a bias-cut lace gown in 1937. Her wedding photographs were developed for twenty-five cents each.

A view of the gown without the slip.

Unusual triangular train.

Back view of Punnett's form-fitting lace gown worn over a double slip of cream satin. *Courtesy of Eileen Punnett.* $650-750.

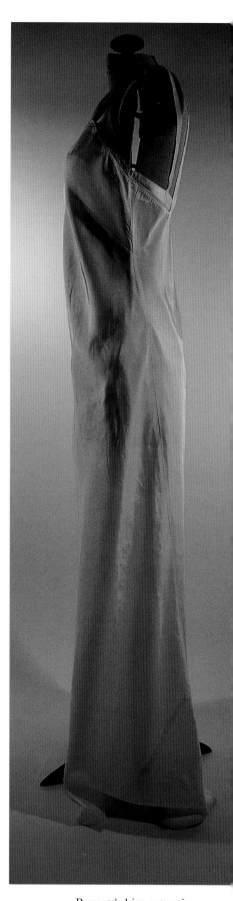

Punnett's bias-cut satin wedding slip has a double-layered skirt to support the lace gown.

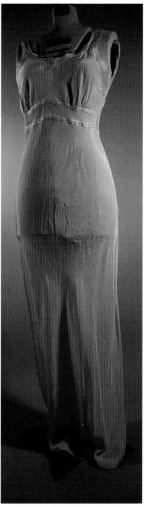

A bridal slip in soft pink similiar to the one on page 88. *Mobile Millinery Museum Collection*. $175-250.

Remodeled wedding gown of Frances Brewis. Original "ashes of roses" *peau-de- soie* skirt was been attached to a brocade bodice and worn as an evening gown. *Courtesy of Joyce Robb*. $200-300.

Ivory rayon wedding gloves with hand smocked detail rise to meet sleeve cuffs.

This satin bra and tap pants, trimmed in floral-patterned lace, were worn by Stella Novak on her wedding day then packed away with the gown, Label: Ideal Maid. *Rachel Kostuk Collection, Mobile Millinery Museum*. $175-225.

Details.

Dress features short full sleeves with double grosgrain bow set against a cascade of chiffon ruches. Sleeves lined with ivory net. Hidden snap closure at cuff.

Stella Novak's 1937 wedding gown of ivory silk chiffon has ruched bodice and four-paneled skirt, which falls from an empire bust line. Scooped neckline if set off with a double grosgrain bow. *Rachel Kostuk Collection, Mobile Millinery Museum*. Ensemble: $800-1000.

Bridal handbag of crocheted silk has been hand sewn to a bakelite handle. Matching change purse. *Mobile Millinery Museum Collection*. $100-150.

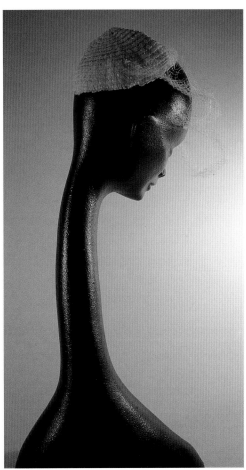

Bride's straw cap with chenille dot veiling. Label: Boyer Exclusive Models, Lachine. *Mobile Millinery Museum Collection*. $45-60.

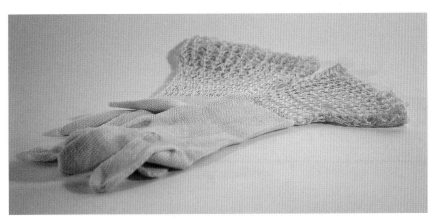

Finely crocheted ecru wedding gloves with lacy cuffs. *Mobile Millinery Museum Collection*. $50-65.

A headpiece of chenille-centered cotton daisies trails a wisp of tulle. *Mobile Millinery Museum Collection*. $125-150.

Chapter Six

1940-1950
War and Post War

Bride Iris Thomas chose a two piece suit of ecru lace and Wedgewood crepe for her wedding to Rev. Norman Hillyer June 12, 1943. Shortie gloves, white Mary Janes, and a tilt hat of blue tulle completed her bridal ensemble.

This pair of seamed nylon stockings has never been worn. The price sticker reads $1.75. *Mobile Millinery Museum Collection.* $35-45.

Throughout the Second World War (1939-1945), fabric rationing, government labor restrictions, economic hardships, and hastily planned weddings had a tremendous impact on bridal style, color, silhouette, embellishment, and accessorization.

Wedding gown designers of the 1940s were likely the most innovative of any fashion decade. Milliners showed particular originality through their distinctive use of fabric remnants to create vertical bridal crowns and coronets or pieced and padded tilt hats.

Long and short gowns took on a military silhouette. Broad shoulders were padded and narrow waists were accentuated with peplums and self-fabric belts. Epaulettes appeared along with fabric-covered buttons. Bodices were pieced to accommodate fabric shortages and the sweetheart neckline, mimicking the shape of a heart, appeared. An off-the-shoulder neckline, or Bertha, was seen in the latter half of the decade and was often enclosed with illusion.

Lace was scarce as production was halted in France during the conflict, leaving wedding gowns largely unadorned. Hand beading and other traditional embellishment techniques were forsaken, as these were labor intensive and designers had to abide by government manhour restrictions. Fingerless gloves, mitts, and gauntlets were a labor saving alternative to the traditional type and a fabric saving alternative to long sleeves. After the war, as factories took time to retool, shortages of raw materials continued in Europe and North America, creating a trend for newly introduced rayon gowns.

Supporting garments were affected by shortages as well. With rubber directed to the war effort, corsets became more structured or were done away with altogether. Stockings, if one could obtain them, were held up by old-fashioned leg garters but a leg film, providing the illusion of stockings, was also available. Silk went into the manufacture of parachutes and cotton was used for duffle bags, leaving brides to refashion heirloom gowns and designers to experiment with non-traditional materials.

In 1947, one British bride was delighted to read an ad in the *Nursing Mirror* which encouraged nurses and midwives like herself to apply for the loan of one of twelve traditional wedding gowns, to be sent from Canada. The former nurse remembers her excitement when the package containing an oyster satin gown arrived. She has no idea who made the gown or how many others wore it before her. After being married in the stylish ensemble, she was only too happy to have it cleaned and redirected to another worthy candidate.

In 1944, wartime restrictions prevented Francis Dawson Jones from obtaining enough fabric to make a traditional wedding dress. In fact her sewing pattern was stamped with a government warning that it was illegal to make up the long view. Undaunted, the ninety-nine pound

Francis Dawson Jones sewing pattern and wedding gown
of drapery net. *Courtesy of Dianne Wood.* $450-500.

Back view of Annette Marcil's pink crepe gown,
which made its debut at 6:30 a.m. August 31,
1940. The gown and accessories were purchased
at Caplan's Department Store in the wedding
section of Ottawa's Rideau Street for $70 tax-
free. *Suzanne Query Collection, Mobile Millinery
Museum.* $500-600.

Prince Edward Island bride took inspiration from Scarlet O'Hara and
created the wedding gown of her dreams – from dotted net curtains.
The drapery fabric could be easily obtained in a large quantity by
pooling ration tickets.

Some brides considered it unpatriotic to be married in a traditional gown. For Annette Marcil, a salmon crepe dress and hat was
just the thing for her 6:30 a.m. wedding to jeweler Maurice Dorion in
1940. There were so many weddings at Marcil's Ottawa Church that
year that priests had to schedule them an hour apart. The smaller the
wedding, the earlier the ceremony. The bride accessorized her gown
with a bouquet of pink roses. Her matching drawstring bag held a
rosary and handkerchief.

Joan Mallet of Woodstock spent twenty-five dollars on her entire
wedding ensemble in 1942. She purchased her white chiffon street-
length dress for five dollars at an end of summer sale. The matching
shoes cost another five and the balance of her budget was lavished on
a hat. A white straw cartwheel with satin trim was the crowning glory
that she remembers fondly to this day.

Padded headpiece of pink crepe has been pieced
from dress fabric remnants. Veil of matching
pink tulle. *Suzanne Query Collection, Mobile
Millinery Museum.* $225.

During the war, bridal parties were small leaving dressmakers and bridal salons with reserves of pastel fabrics, which were made up into wedding gowns. By 1946, with white fabric available and pastels scarce, a short-lived trend developed for the all-white wedding in which a bride and her attendants were similarly attired.

Following the war, surplus parachute silk was sold off inexpensively and much of it went into the construction of wedding gowns. As government restrictions were lifted, satins, silks, brocades, and laces were worn once again.

A war era bride in a short wedding gown of pink georgette.

Open-crown bridal headpiece of pin-tucked georgette has been padded and is lined with rayon satin. With fabrics scarce during the war, some milliners improvised with sanitary pads in lieu of cotton stuffing. *Mobile Millinery Museum Collection*. $60-80.

A post-war "white" wedding. Bride and attendants are similarly attired in white gowns, veils, and headpieces.

Matching pink bridal "slippers" were worn with a short gown of pin-tucked georgette over a rayon satin slip. *Mobile Millinery Museum Collection*. $50-75.

Mary MacLean married Captain Algie Leatham, Feb 3, 1945 in a two-piece ensemble of blue crepe de chine. Her small headpiece was of fabric rose buds. Maid of honor Laurabelle MacLean, was attired in a navy dress and floral tilt hat. The photographer was asked to "add some roses to the bouquet." *Photo by Rapid Grip and Batten Limited, Montreal.*

Bride Jerry Cunningham in a war-era wedding suit and hat accessorized with black pumps and shortie gloves.

Wedding portrait of Mr. and Mrs. Charles MacLean. The groom is in formal attire while the bride wears a simple dress and hat. Hours before the wedding she made a frantic appeal to her future sisters-in-law as something heartbreaking had caused the destruction of her wedding gown.

Three woven straw leaves adorn the crown of this golden tilt hat c. 1942. *Mobile Millinery Museum Collection*. $30-45.

Similar, sleeveless wedding gown of net over satin has classic Greek influence. Neckline, straps and underarms are edged in grape leaves, fashioned from silk ribbon and gold cording. Over-blouse has not survived. *Mobile Millinery Museum Collection*. $400-500.

Opposite page:
Nurse Ethel MacMillan was gowned in white lace and net when she married Optometrist George Stemp July 5, 1941. The bride's fingertip veil of tulle illusion and Mary Queen of Scots headpiece have not survived. *Courtesy of Linda Stemp*. $500-600.

First inset:
Lace jacket with scalloped hem fastens in front with fabric-covered buttons.

Second inset:
Ethel Stemp's wedding gown of satin lined tulle became a ball gown when the lace jacket was removed.

Third inset:
Back view showing delicate tulle edging.

Beige straw adorned with velvet flowers and small turquoise veil – wedding hat of Elda Strasnor, July 27, 1945. *Mobile Millinery Museum Collection.* $50-60.

Satin floral headpiece in Schiaparelli pink with matching veil was worn by a bridesmaid in 1945. *Lois Munz Collection, Mobile Millinery Museum.* $50-75.

Olive green straw going-away hat with orange blossoms and glass balls, c. 1945. *Sara Last Collection, Mobile Millinery Museum.* $100-150.

Opposite page:
Due to rationing and government restrictions in 1943, bride Eleanor Richardson could not obtain bridal satin but was able to procure a bolt of drapery fabric through her cousin, Mae McIntyre, who worked at Eaton's department store in Toronto. This dress of flocked chiffon, was designed and made by McIntyre for Richardson's wedding in 1943. *Mobile Millinery Museum Collection.* $1500-1800.

First inset:
Self-fabric back buttons are decorative only.

Second inset:
Matching Juliet cap of flocked chiffon tops a chapel veil. *Mobile Millinery Museum Collection.* $250-300.

Veil is hand embroidered
in four positions in an
exquisite bow motif.

Self-fabric bow rests below a column of decorative fabric covered buttons.

The chapel veil is gathered onto a coronet headpiece.
Mobile Millinery Museum Collection. $350-400.

Opposite page:
1946 wedding gown of butter-colored damask has princess lines, wedding point sleeves, and sweep train. Left underarm zip. *Mobile Millinery Museum Collection.* $1200-1500.

This bride's simple gown of candlelight satin is enhanced by her "Mary, Queen of Scots" headpiece. *Photo by Kalb Studios, Montreal.*

Back view shows left
underarm zip.

McKinnon's lace-trimmed
veil and headpiece of
nylon tricot rosettes is a
nice complement to
the gown's sweetheart
neckline. $100-150.

Shirley McKinnon's opera length
nylon tricot gloves. $40-50.

Shirley McKinnon's post-war wedding frock of early nylon tricot was purchased at Borden's Ladies Wear, Glace
Bay, Nova Scotia for her nuptials, Wednesday, August 28, 1946. Shoes were difficult to obtain so Shirley wore the
gown with white satin Daniel Green slippers, sent to her from Boston. *Courtesy of Shirley McKinnon.* $350-450.

Trapp's wedding gown with pieced bodice is a fine example of the ingenuity of war-time designers who incorporated fabric remnants into the design of their gowns in order to eliminate waste and meet government regulations. $600-800.

Silk velvet coat lined with candlelight satin hints at Hollywood glamour with it's softly draped collar, velvet buttons, and bow-trimmed pockets. *Anne Miller Collection, Mobile Millinery Museum.* $1500-1800.

Coat lining bears the label of a Canadian department store.

Trapp's coronet headpiece of candlelight satin on a wire frame originally supported a veil of fine net appliquéd with satin wedding bells. It had been borrowed from the bride's sister who received it as a wedding gift from an aunt of the groom. *Anne Miller Collection, Mobile Millinery Museum.* $100-150.

Wedding gown of candlelight satin with sweetheart neckline, wedding point sleeves and attached train worn with red velvet coat by Grace May Trapp, October 12, 1946. Bridesmaid Dorothy Simpson remembers "It rained the day of the wedding. Grace wore the red cape – I envied it. The bridesmaids were given sheets to cover their dresses." *Anne Miller Collection, Mobile Millinery Museum.*

War era gown of slipper satin shown with replica of the bride's prominent corsage. Original ashes of roses color has faded to bronze. Self-fabric belt and covered buckle. *Mobile Millinery Museum collection.* $400-500.

Epaulettes demonstrate military influence on fashion design during the second World War.

Similarly, a bride and maid of honor adorn their suits with
large vertical corsages. *Photo by Kalb Studios, Montreal.*

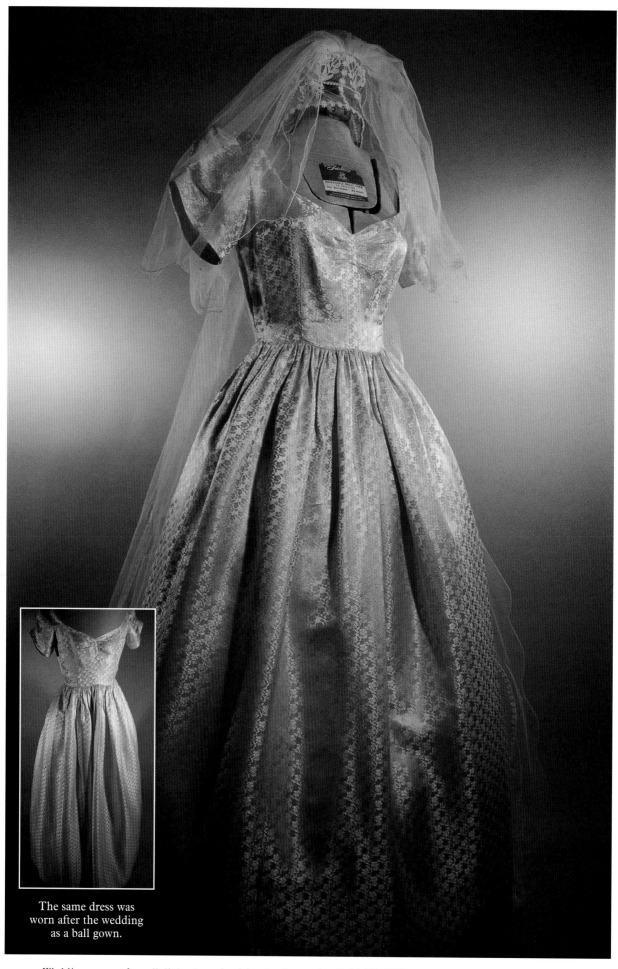

The same dress was
worn after the wedding
as a ball gown.

Wedding gown of candlelight damask with crinoline and veil. *Mobile Millinery Museum Collection.* $600-700.

Eggshell satin gown with yoke of bridal illusion, c. 1948. The sleeves, hem and bodice are trimmed with ecru lace. The lace-trimmed veil has not survived. Mobile *Millinery Museum Collection*. $800-1000.

A bride signs the register in a gown of slipper satin with illusion yoke. *Photo by Kalb Studios, Montreal.*

Knee-length bridal suit of bronze satin has pleated peplum and cutwork bodice. *Mobile Millinery Museum Collection.* $350-400.

Candlelight satin gown boasts a collar beaded with pearls and seed beads.
Seven-foot train, underarm zip. *Mobile Millinery Museum Collection*. $800-1000.

A bride c. 1948 in a satin gown with stand-up collar. *Photo by Kalb Studios.*

C. 1948: these bridesmaids sport satin open-crown hats. *Photo by Kalb Studios, Montreal.*

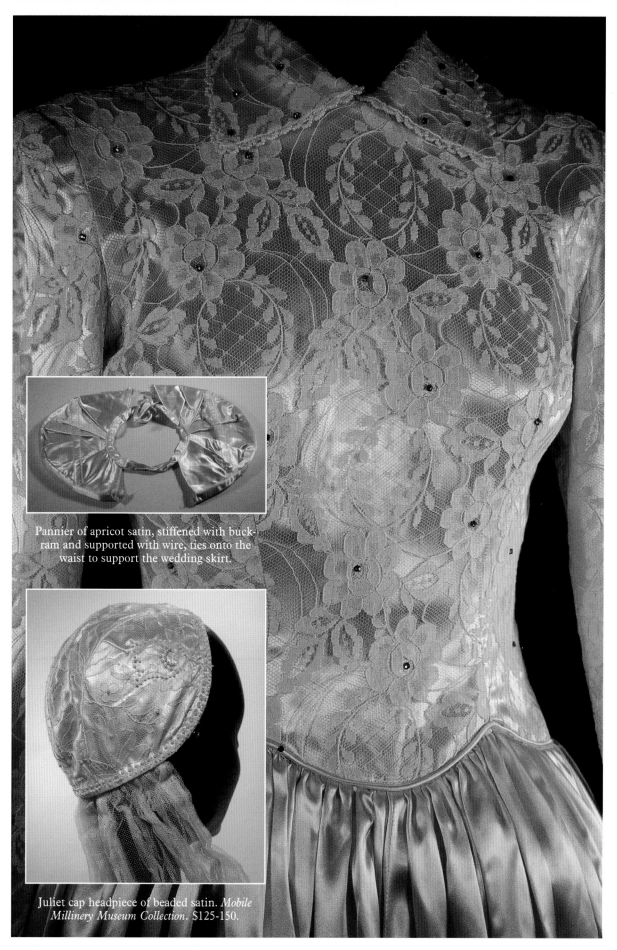

Pannier of apricot satin, stiffened with buckram and supported with wire, ties onto the waist to support the wedding skirt.

Juliet cap headpiece of beaded satin. *Mobile Millinery Museum Collection.* $125-150.

Post-war gown of apricot satin. Basque bodice is overlaid with white, rose-patterned lace and punctuated with set-in rhinestones to simulate dew on flower petals. Collar is edged with seed pearls. The original ensemble included a five-foot train, self-fabric Juliet cap headpiece. *Mobile Millinery Museum Collection.* $1500-1800.

Narrow stand-up collar folds
to border a deep "U" neckline
fitted with pleated panels.
Underarm zip. Self-fabric piping
delineates zigzag waist.

This wedding gown of floral-patterned damask was custom made by Eaton's
department store for one of their catalogue models in the late 1940s. Wedding point
sleeves with seven-button closure. *Mobile Millinery Museum Collection*. $1800-2200.

Seven-foot, attached cathedral train encircles the bride in a pool of watercress damask.

Back view.

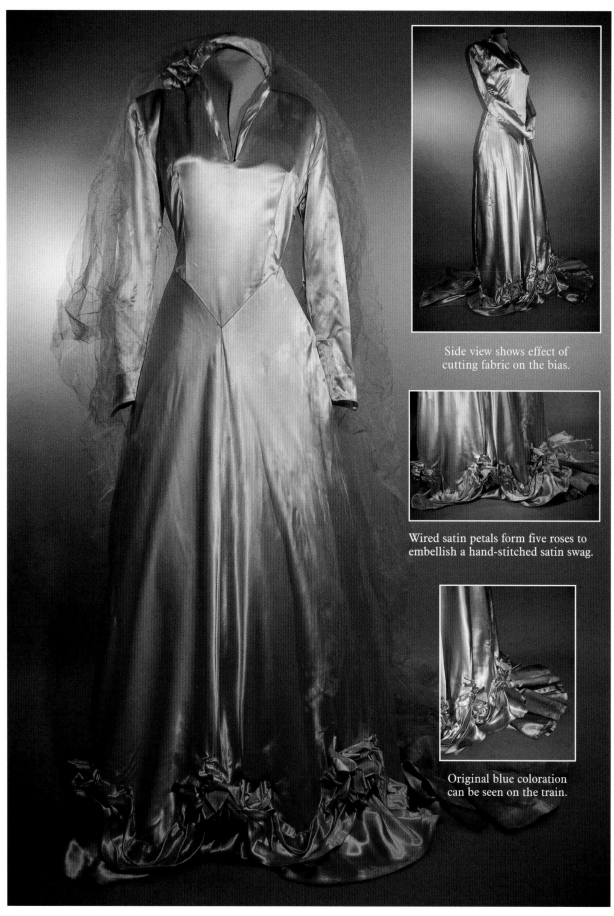

Side view shows effect of cutting fabric on the bias.

Wired satin petals form five roses to embellish a hand-stitched satin swag.

Original blue coloration can be seen on the train.

Powder blue satin wedding gown, inspired by the silver screen, has faded to bronze. Worn with a matching blue tulle veil by blonde bride, Ruth Ann Cooke, September 25, 1948. The dress was made by a friend of the bride, Ruth Sooter who went to Hollywood to work as a fashion designer. By a coincidence, the bride's maiden name was also Ruth Sooter, but no relation. Label: Ruthe Original. *Ruth Cooke Collection, Mobile Millinery Museum.* $2500-3000.

Tulle veil cascades over
padded shoulders and a
rolled collar.

Headpiece of wired satin
roses has faded from
original blue but veil has
retained its color.

Inner view of train reveals an
intricate pattern of tapes, stays and
buckram supports.

Ruth Ann's two-piece
going- away dress of
maroon wool was
originally worn with gray
shoes and purse and a
maroon, bonnet-shaped
hat. *Ruth Cooke Collec-
tion, Mobile Millinery
Museum.* $400-500.

Crescent shaped peplum mirrors the fantail train.

Lace trimmed garter in blue, pink, yellow, and lavender. *Mobile Millinery Museum Collection.* $20-25.

Sheer illusion neckline.

A going away bonnet of orange blossoms is finished with velvet bows. *Mobile Millinery Museum Collection.* $50-65.

Matching bridal mitts with lace cuffs. $45-55.

1949: This ruffled gown with English lace trim and cap sleeves is one of a pair worn by the Stewart sisters in a double wedding in 1949 in Sundridge, Ontario. The groom's gift to bride Kathleen Torell was a brand new car! *Kathleen Torell Collection, Mobile Millinery Museum.* $800-1000.

Chapter Seven

1950–1960
The Barbie Doll Bride

With prosperity, optimism, and women leaving jobs they had held during the war, came a new emphasis on homemaking. Marriage became a career that was idealized in film and the newly developed television. A structured feminine ideal was promoted which involved meticulous grooming and accessorization. 36-26-36 was a numerical code for the perfect woman. Advertisers convinced women that all manner of cosmetics, hair dye, corsets, and props were required to achieve this standard.

Wedding couture followed the formal starched look of everyday fashion. Tulle, which designers had used during the war to embellish hats, was now lavishly applied to wedding gowns and enhanced with generous doses of hand-applied beads, pearls, sequins, and rhinestones. Attached crinolines and layers of stiffened canvas enabled dresses to

Mr. and Mrs. Malcolm MacLean in Brussels on their wedding day, April 25, 1953. Nelly MacLean (nee Giammona) wears a lace wedding coat with chapel train over a strapless ball gown. *Photo by J. Dworkin.*

almost stand up on their own. So popular was this bouffant silhouette that designers topped sheath dresses with removable pumpkin skirts.

Circle and cathedral trains were popular for formal weddings and ballerina and strapless ball-gown styles were selected by brides who did not wish to sport a train. To provide modesty at the altar these were topped with lace, tulle, or chiffon coats and jackets. One 1950s bride even remembers her priest sermonizing on the need for brides to cover bare arms and shoulders during the wedding ceremony.

Merry widow corsets and wired push-up bras were worn beneath the elegant bridal creations of the 1950s to produce cleavage above full skirts and cinched waists. The pointed bust line was popular and spike heels added the finishing touch to a silhouette that defied gravity.

Ballerina gown of machine-embroidered cotton lawn with short sleeves has matching fingerless gloves for a garden party wedding. Many of the remaining buttons, which secure the bodice, have lost their pearly coating. *Mobile Millinery Museum Collection.* $350.

Fingerless gloves fasten with three pearl buttons at the wrist.

Beaded saw-tooth buckram crown with a Statue-of-Liberty effect.

Ballerina gown of rustling Wedgewood taffeta emulates Dior's post-war "New Look" with its rounded shoulders, fitted midriff, and long full skirt. Worn with spiked heels and a small hat by a Toronto area bride. *Mobile Millinery Museum Collection.* $500-600.

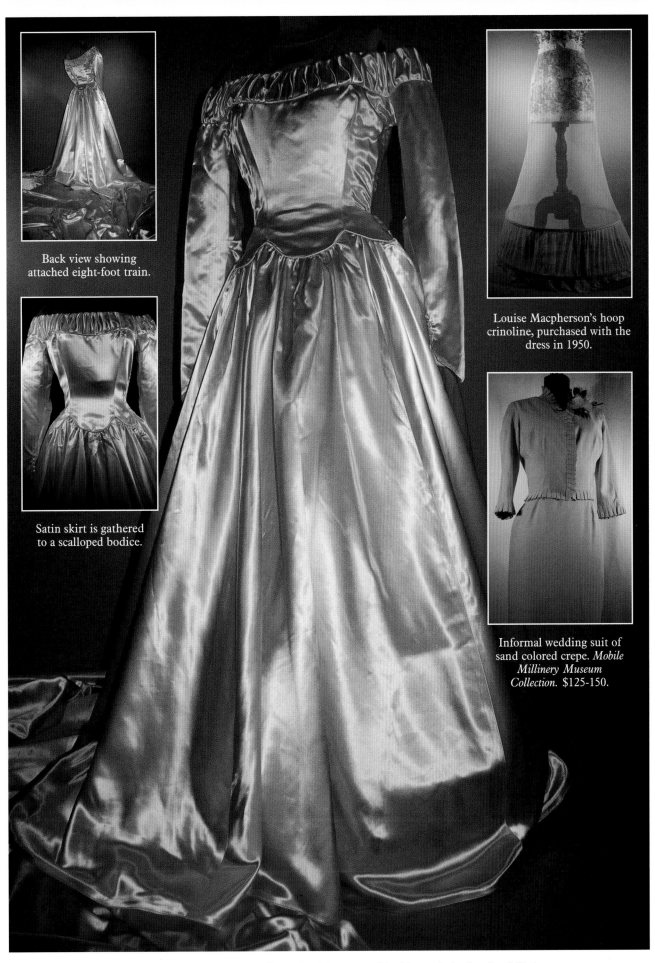

Back view showing
attached eight-foot train.

Satin skirt is gathered
to a scalloped bodice.

Louise Macpherson's hoop
crinoline, purchased with the
dress in 1950.

Informal wedding suit of
sand colored crepe. *Mobile
Millinery Museum
Collection.* $125-150.

Illusion neckline supports an off-the-shoulder gown of ice blue satin by Lord and Taylor.
Worn by Louise Macpherson in 1950. *Mobile Millinery Museum Collection.* $800-1000.

Details.

The edges of a green velvet bow peek out around the waist.

Headpiece of stiffened ecru lace supports a chapel veil.

Narrow split train, resembling ribbon ties, fall at the waist below a large green velvet bow for a St. Patrick's Day bride.

Ecru chantilly lace yokes a high-waisted gown of cream satin, which has been appliquéd with beaded lace and stiffened with pellon. Seed beads outline the neck and sleeve edge. *Mobile Millinery Museum Collection*. $600-800.

Five layers of crimped tulle ruffles support an overskirt of tulle with lace wedges.

Scalloped edge of lace overlay is finished with iridescent sequins.

Ballerina gown with lace overlay bodice has double neckline of folded tulle and voluminous satin lined tulle skirt. Self-fabric back-button closure. Wedding point sleeves of lace and tulle fasten at the wrist with nine fabric-covered buttons. Remnants of confetti are trapped between the bodice and lining. *Mobile Millinery Museum Collection*. $800-1000.

Tulle overlay is gathered onto strips of lace creating a pannier illusion. *Rachel White Collection, Mobile Millinery Museum.* $300-400.

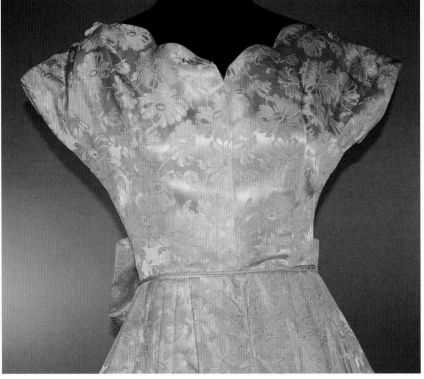

Close-up. Tulle overlay is gathered onto strips of lace creating a pannier illusion

Seven yards of ivory damask went into the construction of this 1950s gown, designed and worn by June Gall. Self-fabric waistline piping, center back zip. *Courtesy of June Gall.* $400-500.

View showing scalloped neckline.

Tulle veil is secured with a millinery rose to match the gown. *Mobile Millinery Museum Collection.* $150-200.

Ballerina gown of tulle and lace over rayon satin has cap sleeves and ruffled tulle neckline. Cerise rose buds punctuate ruffle points. Underarm zip. *Mobile Millinery Museum Collection.* $400-500.

This lace wedding gown with point sleeves and back button closure was designed and worn by bride Connie Price in 1957. The bride carried a prayer book covered in lace to match the overdress and an orchid with ferns caught in trailing ribbon streamers. *Connie Price Collection, Mobile Millinery Museum.* $350-400.

Bride Connie Price in a gown of her own design.

Flyaway tulle veil with blusher is gathered onto a band of stiffened lace. Gold-tone pearl beads are sewn to the band at inner and outer edges, forming a crown. *Connie Price Collection, Mobile Millinery Museum.* $175-225.

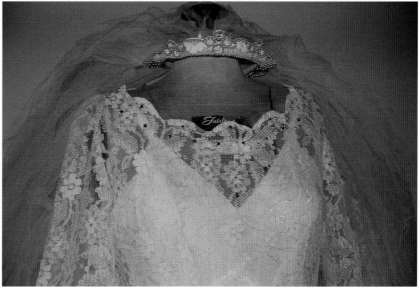

Lace wedding coat with V-neck satin slip.

The full skirt splits at center front with a scalloped edge to reveal a strapless voile gown with hooped crinoline After her marriage, Price wore the under-dress with a red cummerbund and sash to formal dances.

Boned bodice has left side zipper closure and
set-in peek-a-boo bra of ruffled tulle.

Lace overlay ballerina style bodice meets a full-length skirt of tulle
over white satin. *Mobile Millinery Museum Collection*. $350-450.

Satin merry widow and cotton crinoline originally worn with White's gown. $75-100.

Bride Anna Holderson wears a similar gown in 1955.

Lace-trimmed ball gown can be worn under the lace overcoat or alone. Label: Perfect Junior Formal Ltd., Toronto. *Mobile Millinery Museum Collection.*

Pearls and set in rhinestones enhance sweetheart neckline.

Tulle ball gown with lace wedding coat worn by Marion White, July 25, 1955. Bandeau headband and fingertip veil were loaned out and not returned. *Mobile Millinery Museum Collection*. Ensemble: $800-900.

Alternating skirt panels of
tulle and sequined lace.

An early 1950s wedding gown cut down and dyed to become a
cocktail dress. *Mobile Millinery Museum Collection*. $450.

Mother-of-the-bride ensemble in cocoa damask. Bolero jacket with dolman sleeves covers a sleeveless A-line dress. *Eleanor Auld Collection, Mobile Millinery Museum.* Ensemble: $250-350.

Matching close hat with eyebrow veiling and self-fabric hatpin by Toronto milliner Eleanor Auld. Label: Jo-Anne. *Eleanor Auld Collection, Mobile Millinery Museum.*

Princess gown c. 1950. Lace-trimmed full skirt of organza is interlined with net and supported by a set-in crinoline. Bodice of machine lace over organza is lined with satin rayon. Wedding point sleeves and stand-up collar of lace over organza. *Mobile Millinery Museum Collection.* $600-800.

Lace-trimmed full skirt of organza is interlined with net and supported by a fixed crinoline. Organza bows punctuate canter front and back.

Empire waist silk brocade gown for flower girl Marilyn McKinnon c. 1950. Scalloped hem and yolk are each trimmed with self-fabric ruffle and dotted with velvet ribbon bows in soft purple. *Marilyn McKinnon Collection, Mobile Millinery Museum.* $150-200.

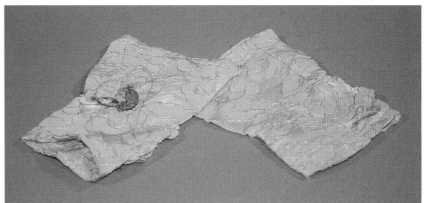

Matching mitts are trimmed with purple velvet bows.

Flower girl Marilyn McKinnon's basket looks identical to the one in photo at right. *Mobile Millinery Museum Collection.* $15-20.

Panels of tulle and lace overlay a satin ball gown worn by bride Phyllis Shierman in 1952. Maid of honor and attendants wear capelets with their ball gowns to cover bare shoulders.

July 27, 1953. Marie Minaker's ballerina length gown has a back button, halter bodice of ivory lace over slipper satin which comes to a point at center front and back over a full skirt of lace-paneled tulle over satin. A lace bolero creates peek-a-boo shoulders and sleeves. *Marie Minaker Collection, Mobile Millinery Museum.* $1200-1500.

Above right:
Bolero accentuates slender midriff.

Center right:
Tulle veil bordered in Brussels lace hangs from a Juliet cap of fine lace on a wire frame. *Marie Minaker Collection, Mobile Millinery Museum.* $200-250.

Right:
Ribbons and dried roses from the bride's original bouquet hang from an underdress with halter bodice.

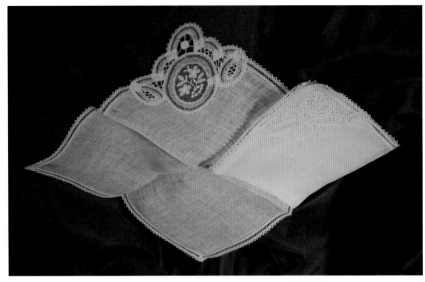

Two bridal hankies of Bruges lace, labeled Dentelles from F. Rubbrecht Co. in Brussels. *Courtesy of Marie Minaker.* $8-12.

A bride in red lipstick signs the register wearing a lace wedding coat and ball gown, 1954. *Photo by Kalb Studios, Montreal.*

A 1950s bride in a lace gown with wedding point sleeves and Juliet cap veil. *Photo by Kalb Studios, Montreal.*

Opposite page, first inset:
A flounce of chiffon separates a yoke of bridal illusion and a chiffon overlay bodice. Lace sleeves.

Second inset:
Center back zipper is hidden beneath faux button closure. Bell skirt of ruffled white organza.

Third inset:
Ruffle motif is repeated on the flyaway veil. *Mobile Millinery Museum Collection.* $50-60.

132

Ruffled polyester chiffon gown supports a nine-foot train. *Mobile Millinery Museum Collection*. $500-600.

A bride in a similar gown carries
her train on a loop of ribbon.

Rosemarie Demers' lace and satin gown accentuates a pointed bust.

An embroidered flyaway veil
falls from a bridal crown,
similar to that of Rosemarie
Demers, above right.

Circle veil dotted with pearls to resemble
confetti rests atop a band braided with
straw cloth and faux pearls. *Mobile
Millinery Museum Collection.* $50-75.

Satin leaves and chain stitch embroidery hem a circle veil beneath a floral
straw bandeau. *Mobile Millinery
Museum Collection.* $75-125.

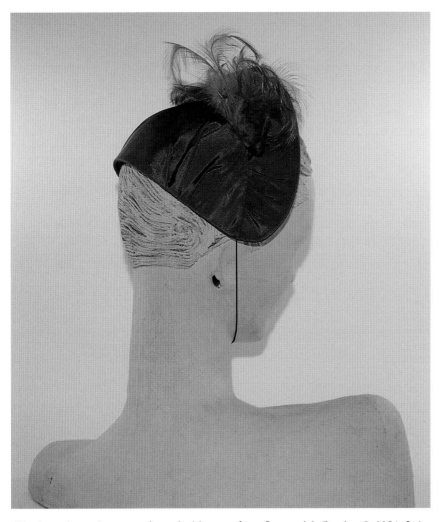

Miniature cloth roses, carnations, and forget-me-nots secure a fine veil to the crown of a bride's shallow pillbox. *Mobile Millinery Museum Collection.* $35-45.

Feather-trimmed green satin revival bonnet for a flower girl, October 9, 1954. *Lois Sutherland Collection, Mobile Millinery Museum.* $60-75.

Going away hat of blue brocade. *Mobile Millinery Museum Collection.* $45-55.

Going-away hat banded in poppies for a November bride. *Mobile Millinery Museum Collection.* $75-85.

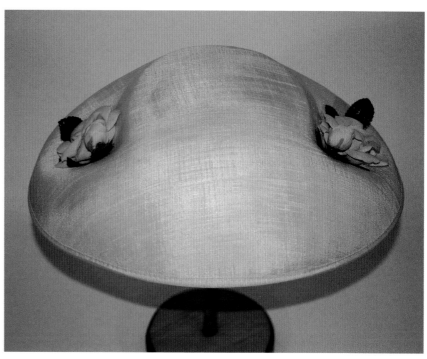

Velvet ribbon bows and blue veiling create a vibrant headpiece for a bridal attendant. *Mobile Millinery Museum Collection.* $50-60.

White silk roses rest on the crown of an ivory linen going-away hat. *Mobile Millinery Museum Collection.* $50-75.

Flyaway veil on a bandeau of straw flowers. *Mobile Millinery Museum Collection.* $50-75.

A bridesmaid's bandeau of brown and turquoise velvet flowers. *Mobile Millinery Museum Collection.* $50-60.

Pink diamond-patterned nylon gloves rest atop a quilted glove box, ready for a bride's getaway. *Mobile Millinery Museum Collection.* $45-55 each.

Crystal and silver beads adorn this bridal handbag. *Mobile Millinery Museum Collection.* $100-150.

Creamy sequined handbag for a 1950s bride. Label: Coronet. *Mobile Millinery Museum Collection.* $75-100.

Silk bridal bag has lift clasp and rhinestone studded frame. *Mobile Millinery Museum Collection.* $75-100.

Shortie gloves with alternating pearls and rhinestones for a 1950s bride. *Mobile Millinery Museum Collection.* $60-75.

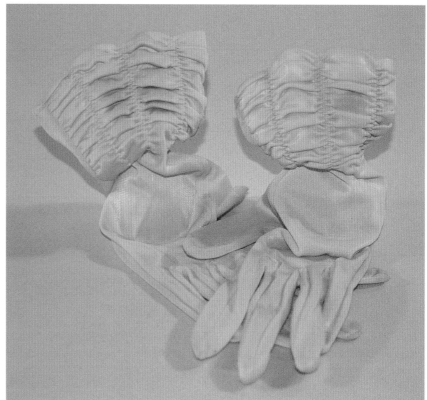

Nylon shortie gloves. Label: Nylon by Austin.
Mobile Millinery Museum Collection. $35.

1950s hankie of flocked chiffon for a Valentine bride.
Mobile Millinery Museum Collection. $8-12.

Top left:
Elbow length wedding gloves to match an ashes-of-roses
gown, rest in their original package. Label: Paris Gloves.
Mobile Millinery Museum Collection. $35-45.

Center left:
Pink lace trousseau penoir with marabou collar and cuffs.
Mobile Millinery Museum Collection. $125-150.

Left:
Rose-patterned chiffon hankie carried by a 1950s bride.
Mobile Millinery Museum Collection. $8-12.

Chapter Eight

1960-1970
The Second Women's Movement

The 1960s was a decade of renewed political activism for women. As they advocated for equality in the workplace, many defied social convention and discarded corsets, bras, and impossible shoes. Girdles vanished and pantyhose made the scene. Free-spirited brides of the hippie movement, c. 1964-1970, were married in bare feet with flowers in their hair and some designers went so far as to create a nude look.

Skirt dimensions had reached tremendous proportions in the previous decade and could only contract. The first to go was the pumpkin skirt. A slim silhouette was well established by 1965. Short wedding gowns followed the mini skirt craze and enjoyed a brief period of popularity. Brides had a choice of opera length or shortie gloves to wear with cap-sleeved and short-sleeved dresses.

Detachable trains returned and fell from the shoulder, bust line or waist, enhancing A-line and sheath silhouettes that rested at the ankle to reveal satin pumps dyed to match bride's and attendants' wedding gowns. Chantilly over taffeta was popular with brides who wanted to rustle as they made their way down the aisle but it was also paired with satin or brocade. Skirts interlined with pellon® for its stiffening effect, ensured a quieter procession.

Millinery designers created crown and pillbox-styled headpieces that spewed flyaway and fingertip veiling atop empire-waisted gowns. Revival bonnet or bathing cap headpieces were seen for a short time but were not widely adopted.

Daisies were popular and flower trimmed going-away hats a must. Dresses and hair adornments for attendants mimicked those for the bride but were made up in pastel hues or muted shades of rust, brown, and green.

Traditional brides opted to have their hair coiffed into a beehive, flip, pageboy, chignon, or French twist. Salons everywhere were freely imitating the bouffant styles created for celebrities and models by New York hairdresser Michel Kazan. Brides topped false lashes with blue eye shadow and tried out wigs, falls, and other hairpieces, often in platinum blonde.

Scalloped lace forms an apron over
a *peau-de-soie* A-line skirt.

The blonde Chantilly lace for the gown's overlay
came from Switzerland. *Roberta Brooks Collection, Mobile Millinery Museum.* $800-1000.

Roberta Brooks paid $600 for her wedding gown at Eaton's Department Store in
Toronto for her marriage Thursday, April 15, 1965. As a teacher she had Easter
week off for her honeymoon and was married at 7:30 p.m. on the previous Thursday evening so as not to interfere with choir practice at the church.

Creamy silk tulle veil is anchored by a silk
and velvet cabbage rose, made by the bride's
mother-in-law. This style of headpiece was
known to milliners as a miners cap. *Mobile
Millinery Museum Collection.* $100-150.

140

Betty Gibson's floor length gown of white organza over taffeta was worn in July, 1961 with a crown of matching Chantilly lace and shoulder-length veil. The skirt, designed of four box pleats, was stiffened with Pellon® and appliquéd with Chantilly lace to match the bodice. *Courtesy of Elizabeth Sanders.* $600-800.

Mini-dress wedding gown from January, 1963 has lace overlay bodice and full skirt of candlelight satin, lined with Pellon™. *Marilyn McKinnon Collection, Mobile Millinery Museum.* $300-400.

Mrs. Marie Phillips chose to wear a mini dress for her nuptials in 1963.

C. 1968: A long sleeved straight cut wedding gown of guipure lace over a flesh-toned lining pays homage to the nude look. *Mobile Millinery Museum Collection*. $500-600.

Ruffles add interest to this polyester crepe wedding gown and satin bridesmaid's dress. Each have center back zip and bodice detail of fabric-covered buttons. *Mobile Millinery Museum Collection*. Each: $300-400.

The richness of the fabric softens the severe lines of this gown.

A-line gown of winter-white twill with zippered sleeves is simply trimmed at the neck with lace, white seed beads and silver bugles. Silver beads on the garland headpiece have tarnished. *Mobile Millinery Museum Collection.* $250-300.

Lace sleeves and a diagonal lace yoke add contrast.

Machine embroidered florals on white duchesse satin make up the body of this sleek 1960s gown. Satin bow marks center front, knee to ankle side pleats allow movement. *Mobile Millinery Museum Collection*. $350-400.

White chantilly overlays bust and completes the sleeves. Set-in rhinestones anchor loops of miniature pearl beads, which fall at the nipple line and between.

Detachable watteau train is appliquéd with white chantilly.

A bride of the 1960s in a short-sleeved gown with similar neckline.

Short sleeved gown of white satin crepe with empire line has hook-and-eye closure over off-center back zip. *Mobile Millinery Museum Collection*. $500-600.

This ivory taffeta gown is lined with Pellon™ and supported by a stiff crinoline set into the construction of the skirt. Label: Perfect Junior, Toronto. Purchased by Ruth Norton at Sears, 1964. *Mobile Millinery Museum Collection*. $450-550.

Pearl-beaded lace outlines sleeves, front panel, and attached train.

Joan Norton's pillbox headpiece and veil. *Mobile Millinery Museum Collection*. $100-150.

Bride Marg Cashmore's 1960s wedding headpiece of cream satin with self-fabric leaves originally had a two-tiered veil and was made by her mother to match the cream satin wedding gown. The blonde bridal attendants each wore a bronze diadem. *Marg Cashmore Collection, Mobile Millinery Museum.* $45-65.

Margaret Cashmore in a short-sleeved A-line wedding dress, 1966.

A bridesmaid's veiled diadem in avocado green. *Marg Cashmore Collection, Mobile Millinery Museum.* $25-50.

A delicate watteau train falls from a voile overlay gown, appliquéd with leaf-patterned lace. Bride: Phyllis Cheeseman, 1965. *Mobile Millinery Museum Collection*. $400-500.

A short veil appliquéd with similar lace falls from a crown of crystal beads. $75-100.

Phyllis Cheeseman's garter lays atop the hem of her voile overlay gown with appliquéd lace.

Phyllis Cheesemans's ribbon and lace garter is adorned with fabric blue bells, paste hearts, a silver wedding bell, and star sequins.

Registry office wedding dress of buttery crepe c. 1968. Overdress of daisy-patterned lace with three-quarter sleeve is bound at the neck, hem, and sleeve with matching satin. This ensemble was worn originally with go-go boots. *Mobile Millinery Museum Collection.* $400-500.

A bride's going away suit c. 1968 consists of a sleeveless A-line dress and shortie jacket. *Mobile Millinery Museum Collection.* $250-300.

Beaded buttons add interest to jacket front detail, which appears as an extension of bound buttonholes.

Organza skirt is supported by net, nylon and buckram. Quarter-inch lavender ribbon bands neck, waist, and hem.

Four bands of machine lace run from neck to hem accentuating the straight lines of this sleeveless wedding gown c. 1970. Organza bodice is lined with a double thickness of white nylon. *Mobile Millinery Museum Collection.* $400-500.

A crown of silk flowers on a fabric braid encircles a crown of lavender veiling. *Mobile Millinery Museum Collection.* $75-125.

Pink synthetic chiffon overlays a bridesmaid's gown of matching nylon fabric. Empire bodice, waist, and cuff bands have been machine embroidered. Ruffled stand-up collar and cuffs add a feminine touch to this dress, which completely covers the female form. *Mobile Millinery Museum Collection.* $150-200.

Flocked chiffon in a floral centered medallion pattern for a bridesmaid's dress c. 1965.

High-crowned gold brocade hat with black velvet band and pleated brim worn by Sara Last on the occasion of her second marriage, to complement a gold mini dress and shoes. *Mobile Millinery Museum Collection.* $85-125.

1966 empire wedding gown of candlelight satin, lined with Pellon™, has net underskirt and wedding point sleeves. Wide band of heavy machine lace provides a contrast in texture and design. Chapel train attaches at shoulder with double bows. *Georgi Haner Collection, Mobile Millinery Museum.* Ensemble: $400-500.

Baby doll trousseau set of corn colored nylon has sleeves and jacket of alternating crimped chiffon ruffles and bands of machine embroidery. Covered button closure, neck and center fronts edged in picot trim. *Mobile Millinery Museum Collection.* $100-150.

Georgi Haner's trousseau nightgown of white lace and pink chiffon, 1966. *Courtesy of Georgi Haner.* $40-50.

Bride's going-away hat of pink horsehair ribbon. *Mobile Millinery Museum Collection.* $50-75.

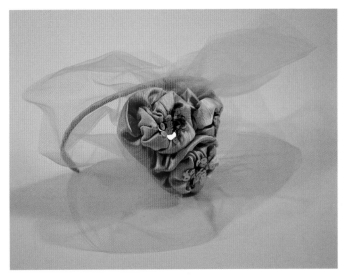

This gold trefoil bridesmaid's hat made its debut in November, 1962. Confetti is still trapped within the veiling. *Lois Sutherland Collection, Mobile Millinery Museum.* $50-75.

Stiffened lace headpiece on wire frame by Philip Warde. When Elizabeth Taylor married actor Richard Burton in Montreal in 1964, she turned to this Toronto designer for her white and yellow cascading floral headpiece. *Philip Warde Collection, Mobile Millinery Museum.* $250-300.

Chantilly lace adorns a slender *peau-de-soie* gown c. 1965. A tapered train falls from self-fabric bows at the shoulder. Label: David E. Rae, Toronto. *Mobile Millinery Museum Collection.* $400-500.

Patricia Boyle selected a headpiece of petals and stamens to anchor her flyaway veil. *Mobile Millinery Museum Collection.* $150.

Iridescent sequins cap two vertical columns of lace on an organza overlay gown worn by teacher Patricia Boyle July 7, 1962. *Mobile Millinery Museum Collection.* $350-400.

Pearl studded red velvet diadem for a valentines bride. *Mobile Millinery Museum Collection.* $25-35.

Daisy trimmed diadem with matching circle veil for a 1960s bridesmaid. *Mobile Millinery Museum Collection.* $45-55

Flyaway veil of white tulle falls from a miner's cap of white fabric roses and lily-of-the-valley. *Mobile Millinery Museum Collection.* $150-200.

A double circle of tulle falls from a bridesmaid's peach chiffon bow. *Mobile Millinery Museum Collection.* $25-35.

Flyaway veil on a band of orange blossoms. *Mobile Millinery Museum Collection.* $50-75.

A silk floral headpiece c. 1960, designed to envelop a topknot of upswept hair, supports a gathered flyaway veil. *Mobile Millinery Museum Collection.* $125.

In lieu of veiling, a bride's revival bonnet secures with ribbon under the chin to complement a ruffled wedding gown. *Mobile Millinery Museum Collection.* $75-100.

A flyaway veil and blusher are swept up to perch from a floral crown. *Mobile Millinery Museum Collection.* $50-75.

An embroidered circular veil on a crown of wired chenille. *Mobile Millinery Museum Collection.* $45-55.

A junior bridesmaid's daisy-trimmed
bandeau. *Mobile Millinery Museum
Collection.* $60-75.

A multitude of tiny pink flowers add
texture to this pink taffeta headband,
worn by a bride's attendant c. 1965. *Mobile
Millinery Museum Collection.* $45-60.

Blue satin pillbox and matching drawstring bag for a maid of honor. *Mobile
Millinery Museum Collection* Blue. $75-100.

A bridesmaid's bandeau brimming with
turquoise forget-me-nots. *Mobile Millinery
Museum Collection.* $75-100.

A bride's going-away hat and gloves. Floral trimmed cone-hat bears a
Paris label: Lucyane. *Mobile Millinery Museum Collection.* $150.

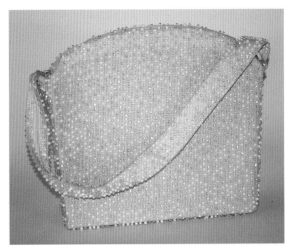

Bride's handbag c. 1960. White and
transparent beads on eggshell canvas.
Mobile Millinery Museum Collection. $30.

Rhinestone centered rosettes sit atop a
vinyl coated clutch purse. *Mobile Millinery
Museum Wedding Collection.* $50-65.

Creamy veiled bandeau of woven straw, a bride's going away
hat c. 1965. *Mobile Millinery Museum Collection.* $60-75.

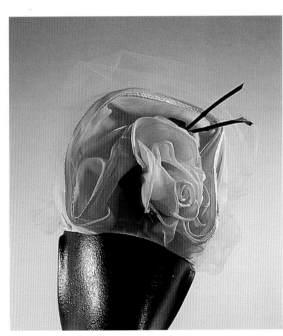

Mother-of-the-bride: Stripes of narrow
straw band pink organza, which has been
folded to simulate ribbon. A silk and
velvet rose punctuates the back of this
turbanesque bubble toque by
Schiaparelli. *Mobile Millinery Museum
Collection.* $125-150.

Yoke and sleeves entirely of lace.

A pencil straight gown of synthetic crepe with watteau train. *Mobile Millinery Museum Collection*. $250-350.

A bride c. 1968 in a going-away suit and high crowned hat.

Chenille-centered daisies band a straw honeymoon hat c. 1968. *Mobile Millinery Museum Collection*. $60-80.

An avocado velvet bow resets on a daisy strewn hat by Irene of Montreal. *Mobile Millinery Museum Collection*. $125-150.

A milliner has added flowers to the crown and raspberry tulle to the brim of a high crowned pink straw for a bride's going away ensemble c. 1968. *Mobile Millinery Museum Collection.* $85.

This bride's going away hat is almost a reverse of the one at left. *Mobile Millinery Museum Collection.* $60-80.

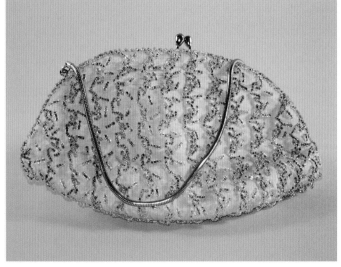

A white silk bridal bag adorned with silver beads. *Mobile Millinery Museum Collection.* $60-80.

This bridal bag with gold-tone chain handle glistens with iridescent sequins. *Mobile Millinery Museum Collection.* $50-60.

Chapter Nine

1970–1980
That Seventies Wedding

Wedding gowns of the 1970s are distinctive and easily recognized for their medieval appearance, insubstantial weight, and hand-clipped lace embellishments. As hippie styles and street wear became more mainstream, the A-line silhouette of the previous decade disappeared and designers opted for a romantic fluid look, reminiscent of the middle ages.

The wide use of synthetics in wedding design during the 1970s produced gowns that are lightweight and washable. Most have high necklines, long bell-shaped sleeves, and a center back zip. Designers experimented with the new nylon fabrics now available to them, clipping and gluing lace embellishments to necklines, sleeves, trains, and veils.

Hairstyles for brides became as loose and flowing as the gowns they were paired with. Nylon skirts were overlaid with organza or chiffon. Matching trains floated down the aisle.

Bodices retained the empire waistlines of the sixties but were joined to camelot sleeves and ample skirts with deep, dust-ruffle flounces. Square or rectangular veils, up to nine feet in length, cascaded from the back of the head. Alternatively, these romantic gowns were topped with wide-brim horsehair pamelas, which had not been seen since the twenties.

The author receives wedding guests in an ice blue crepe wedding gown and veiled open-crown hat, August 25, 1973. She and her attendants each wear their hair long and flowing in keeping with the 1970s "natural" look.

A veiled open-crown is dotted with lace posies and edged in braid.

Beading was applied on top of lace trimming in an attempt to create a neo-Victorian appearance. Even parasols made a second debut. Donna Young remembers carrying a lace-trimmed nylon sunshade when she served as a bridesmaid for her friend Trudy Pate in 1973. Young and Pate's other two bridal attendants carried the parasols over the shoulder in the open position while processing down the aisle and throughout the ceremony.

Many informal and/or free spirited brides of the seventies kept step with street styles and were married in everything from hand-knit gowns to hot pants and jumpsuits. Toward the end of the decade, a moderate country-girl look became popular. In July 1978 Elizabeth Hillyer chose a Victorian-inspired simple batiste gown for her wedding in the country. The high-waisted gown with deep V-neck is lined with rayon satin and ornamented with machine lace and quarter-inch satin ribbon at the neckline, cuffs and dust ruffles. A self-fabric sash allows for a generous bow when tied at the back. In lieu of a veil, the bride wore a spray of fresh flowers (daisies and blue mums) in her hair.

A tulle veil with blusher rises vertically from a lace border then drops to cathedral length. *Mobile Millinery Museum Collection.* $150-175.

Powder blue nylon parasol with imitation bamboo handle of the type favored by some 1970s bridal attendants. C. 1973. *Mobile Millinery Museum Collection.* $50-75.

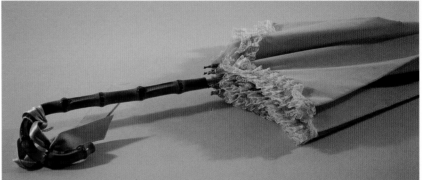

Mr. and Mrs. DeLuca were married at the bride's country home July 29, 1978.

Bride Elizabeth DeLuca with her father, Rev. Hillyer, who performed the marriage ceremony.

This chiffon-overlay nylon gown typifies the bridal silhouette of the early 1970s. A chapel veil with blusher is hemmed in lace to match the gown. *Mobile Millinery Museum Collection.* $600-750.

Elizabeth Hillyer's wedding gown of cornflower organdie with self-fabric sash and white machine lace at cuffs and neckline has deep dust ruffle hem. $200-250.

Back view, as above.

Similar gown of sandalwood organdie, trimmed with picot lace and satin ribbon was purchased the same year at a Toronto lingerie shop for $85 by bride Corey Brooks. Eight faux pearl buttons open a bib front of machine-embroidered organdie. Center back zipper. Label: Shamish &Yofi. *Courtesy of Corey Johnston.* $200-250.

Floral medallions hem a veil of tulle to complement a soft white gown with bridal collar and illusion neckline. *Courtesy of Deb Foley.* Ensemble: $450-550.

A border of lace also serves as a headpiece for a chapel veil c. 1975. *Mobile Millinery Museum Collection.* $200-250.

A deluge of chiffon cascades from an empire waist. Attached chapel train. Matching lace-trimmed veil. *Mobile Millinery Museum Collection.* $600-700.

The bodice and attached train of this chiffon overlay short-sleeved gown are graced with pink ruffles and white lace tulips. *Mobile Millinery Museum Collection.* $450.

Complementary pamela of pink synthetic horsehair. *Edith Mitchell Collection. Mobile Millinery Museum.* $45-55.

Bands of braid cover seam
lines and add interest to this similarly-styled
dress.

Chiffon overlay nylon gown with detachable chapel train. *Mobile Millinery Museum Collection.* $350-450.

Matching lace fan adds a touch
of Victoriana. Mobile Millinery
Museum collection. $25-30.

The bodice of this sleeveless gown is overlaid with fine machine lace. *Mobile Millinery Museum Collection.* $300-350.

A Camelot headpiece. Veil is edged in braid and extends to 108 in. *Mobile Millinery Museum Collection.* $150-200.

A face-framing headpiece of snow-white lace supports a fingertip veil. *Mobile Millinery Museum Collection.* $200-250.

Designers of the seventies favored attached trains.

Unusual gown of white polyester crepe has yoke, upper sleeve and deep dust ruffle of drapery-weight lace. Accordion-pleated skirt and lower sleeve, ruffled collar and yoke detail, center back zip. *Mobile Millinery Museum Collection*. $350-400.

This sleeveless wedding gown of drapeable jersey knit was selected for its simplicity by bride Judy Pollard Smith in 1976. The dress, lined with a bias stretch nylon has center back zip and an original price tag of forty dollars. *Courtesy of Judy Pollard Smith*. $300-400.

The satin ribbon on this two-tiered veil complements the synthetic straw picture hat, woven to look like ribbon. *Mobile Millinery Museum Collection*. $125.

Fingertip veil on a wired bandeau is trimmed with a wide band of machine lace and a double row of narrow lace trim. *Mobile Millinery Museum Collection*. $150-200.

This grass green gown and jacket of jersey knit for a mother-of-the-bride c. 1976 is made special by its matching feather collar. Label: Algo. *Mobile Millinery Museum Collection*. $400-500

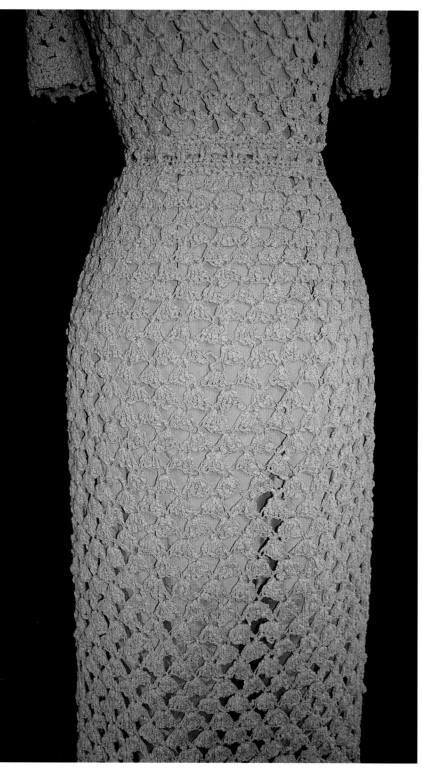

In April, 1973 bride Jean Allen retired from her position as chief librarian at Toronto's legislative library and was married. She selected a green crochet wedding dress to do double duty at parties and receptions. The full-length short-sleeved crochet dress with drawstring waist is worked by hand and worn over a slip of matching satin rayon. Label: Parlour Clothing Company. *Mobile Millinery Museum Collection*. $600-800.

The body of this Swiss dot bridesmaid's gown of golden yellow is lined with rayon satin and banded at the empire waist with satin ribbon. Cream lace at neck, cuffs and dust ruffle has deepened in color with age. *Mobile Millinery Museum Collection.* $200-250.

This daisy-print organza overlay, lined with polyester satin and topped with a self-fabric duster, was chosen by a free-spirited bride for a registry office wedding c. 1973. Label: The House of Nu-Mode, Toronto. *Mobile Millinery Museum Collection.* $400-500.

The cheery dress makes a rustling sound when worn.

High, crossover bodice is underlined
with a band of broad, velvet ribbon.

The circular sleeves and collar of this dotted print
organdie mimic its deep dust ruffle hem. Nylon
lining is robin's egg blue. Bridesmaid's gown c.
1973. *Mobile Millinery Museum Collection*. $350-400.

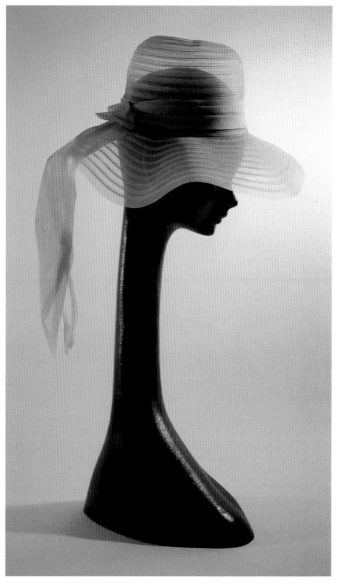

A bridesmaid's horsehair straw hat with organdie band
and bow. *Mobile Millinery Museum Collection*. $50-60.

Floral print chiffon covers the brim of this nylon bridesmaid's
hat, c.1973. *Mobile Millinery Museum Collection*. $65-75.

A peach of a bridesmaid's hat in chiffon and
horsehair straw. *Mobile Millinery Museum
Collection*. $65-75.

Bride Donna Young spotted this horsehair pamela at a millinery shop next door to where she purchased her gown. *Courtesy of Donna Young.* $60-80.

This empire gown of lace trimmed snowy white cotton cost the bride $165 in 1974. Label: Alfred Angelo. *Courtesy of Donna Young.* $350-450.

Jan Nagloren's wedding bouquet with its trail of ribbons and rosebuds is the perfect complement to the clean outline of her wedding skirt.

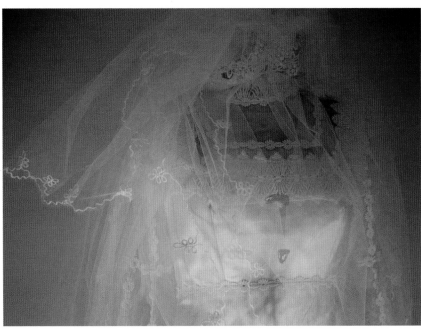

Jan Nagloren's blusher veil sweeps the shoulders of her transparent sleeves. *Courtesy of Jan Nagloren.* $80-100.

Camelot headpiece takes embroidered veil to new heights. *Mobile Millinery Museum Collection.* $60-80.

Bride Cecile Lecavallier's crescent headpiece achieves vertical interest with a spray of marabou on December 27, 1976.

A column of fabric-covered buttons emerges from below a self-fabric bow.

Medium weight crepe gown with detachable train falling from just below the shoulder blades.
Flyaway veil hemmed with lace cord. *Mobile Millinery Museum Collection*. $450-500.

Rose-patterned lace delineates the bust and shoulders of this cream organza overlay c. 1974. Miniature faux pearls form a lattice pattern at the yoke and dot the stand-up collar. Label: Avida Boutique, David E. Rea, Toronto, Canada. *Mobile Millinery Museum Collection.* $400-500.

A buckram cap, enclosed in lace and organza supports a chapel veil. *Mobile Millinery Museum Collection.* $150-200.

Halter-top jumpsuit of guipure lace over grape cotton. A ruffle of lace softens the deep V-neckline. *Mobile Millinery Museum Collection.* $175-225.

Liesje VanZwol's wedding gown is overlaid with machine lace and dotted with pearl beads. Label: Party Time Fashions Ltd., Toronto. Center back zip. Court train. *Mobile Millinery Museum Collection.* $300-350.

Liesje VanZwol's bridal hat was purchased at a department store and festooned with bridal lace. *Mobile Millinery Museum Collection.* $60-80.

Chapter Ten

1980–1990
The Power Bride

The design industry's love affair with nylon was short lived. A multitude of synthetic fabrics became available in the eighties, including many that produced a heavy sheen. Beads, sequins, and pearls were used as embellishments for bridal gowns that were large and lavish. In contrast to these were matte-textured gowns of double knit with form-fitting bodices.

It was the decade of the working woman's "power suit" and a wide silhouette with heavily padded shoulders was both seen at the office and integrated into wedding fashion. Sleeves expanded to enormous proportions. A less popular contrasting look developed out of the 1980s craze for fitness. The enthusiasm for dancewear was so great that some women were loath to give up their cotton and Lycra blends even for a trip down the aisle. They wore heavy double knit gowns with close fitting sleeves.

The handkerchief hem returned on drop-waisted gowns that fell to mid calf. These were popular with brides who married late in life or who took a second trip down the aisle. Bridal salons also offered knee-length dress and jacket combinations. Detachable trains disappeared.

Cap veils were seen but many brides chose to balance broad shouldered gowns with lacy wedding hats. Brims diminished in size from the previous decade and might be turned up on one side or the other. Veiling was often incorporated into the design of the hat. Tulle trailed from the back or side of wedding hats and blushers vanished.

Silk posies replaced fresh flowers in wedding bouquets with brides-to-be often making their own. Gloves disappeared but draw-string bridal bags with over-the-shoulder straps were sometimes worn.

A beaded gown of crystalette with matching drawstring bag. *Mobile Millinery Museum Collection.* $400-500.

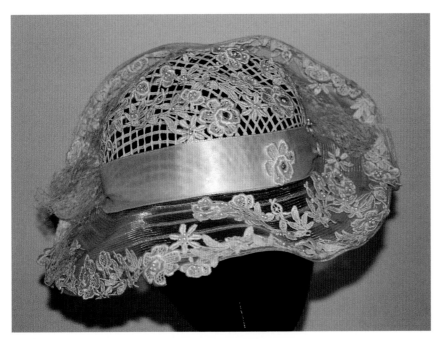

A bridal hat and veil, typical of the 1980s; chiffon over brim, lace embellishments, pearl beading. $150-200.

Satin scallops at bust line
float over a yoke of
patterned machine lace
simulating scales.

Goddess of the Sea.
Unusual hooded
gown of heavy white
satin, backed with
organza and
supported by a net
underskirt.. *Mobile
Millinery Museum
Collection.* $600-800.

Back view. Hood
transforms into a deep
satin swag.

Hood attaches to gown at
the shoulders with self-
fabric buttons.

A circular train emerges beneath a scalloped satin hem to encircle the bride in a puddle of lace.

Side view.

Cathi Gunn's bouquet of silk roses looks as fresh today as it did in 1985. shown with the bride's organza overlay gown and fingertip veil. Ensemble: $350-450.

Hand-clipped lace embellishes a buckram crown, horsehair brim, and satin band to complete a 1980s bridal hat. *Mobile Millinery Museum Collection*. $60-80.

A heavy gown of polyester double knit with lace embellishments. *Mobile Millinery Museum Collection.* $250-350.

Carole Minaker's chiffon covered horsehair picture hat with fingertip veil is adorned with spring flowers to harmonize with the bouquet. *Mobile Millinery Museum Collection.* $225.

A bridal hat of polyester double knit on a buckram crown and wired brim trails tulle veiling to harmonize with the gown above. *Mobile Millinery Museum Collection.* $50-60.

Carole Minaker's open-toed lace wedding shoes. *Minaker Collection, Mobile Millinery Museum.* $35-45.

Bride Carole Minaker in a wedding gown of sleek synthetic lace June 16, 1984. *Photo by Terry White.*

Minaker's silk bouquet has been preserved together with a University of Calgary catering services invoice for $1875. *Mobile Millinery Museum Collection.* $35-45.

Pink silk flowers and a pouf of tulle on a pink satin bow makes an unusual head-piece for a bridal attendant. Worn June 16, 1984. *Minaker Collection, Mobile Millinery Museum.* $35-45.

Carole Minaker straight cut gown is atypical. *Mobile Millinery Museum Collection* $450-550.

Informal wedding gown of polyester silk has double sleeve and hem, reminiscent of Edwardian styling. *Mobile Millinery Museum Collection.* $250-300.

Machine lace borders a skirt and underskirt.

Back view. Machine embroidered lace drapes softly at V neck, sleeve, under sleeve and hem.

Tasseled medallion of translucent bugle beads hands from breastplate to waist.

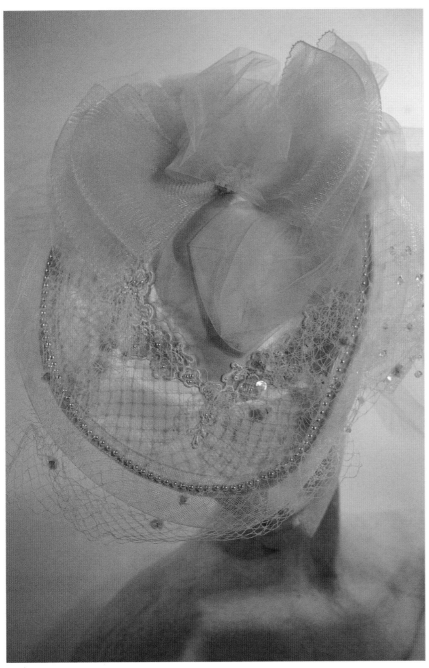

Vanilla chiffon-overlay for New Years Eve bride, Paulette Smith, has blouson bodice, padded sleeve caps and mid-calf hemline, features typical of the 1980s power-femme look. Machine embroidered appliqués are studded with pearl beads and iridescent sequins. Label: Blue Bird Dress, Toronto. *Mobile Millinery Museum Collection.* $300-350.

As above. Elaborate wedding hat with three-tiered spray of silk tulle veiling. Satin-covered brim is turned up on the left to reveal a horsehair bow with crystal antennae, narrow floral braid, and an under-crown of satin-covered buckram. A lace appliqué of pearls and iridescent sequins bands the crown and supports a chenille-dotted veil. Horsehair band extends the brim, horsehair bow at center back. $200-250.

View of neckline and veiled wedding hat.

Rachel Query signed her maiden name for the last time when she was married in a lace overlay wedding gown on May 10, 1986. Query's attached chapel train fell from a satin bow at the waist back and terminated in matching detail at the hem.

Rachel Query's lace overlay wedding gown. View showing satin bow at center back. *Mobile Millinery Museum Collection*. $600-800.

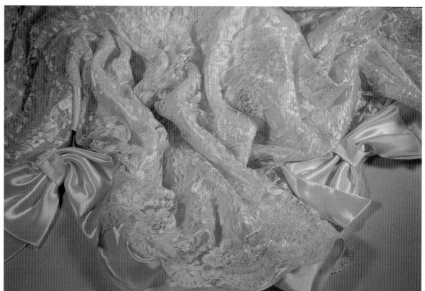

View of hemline showing satin bows.

Plastic cake topper with silver server. Topper: $25-35.

Matching beaded cap and veil.

This dramatic 1980s gown has center-back pearl button closure. The deep illusion neckline is accentuated by heavily sequined machine embroidered panels, which visually extend the shoulders. The crystalette overskirt is supported by three layers of tulle and is separated from the bodice by a procession of faux pearl clusters. *Mobile Millinery Museum Collection*. $500-600.

Elongated Juliet cap trails a narrow veil. This style was popularized by Princess Dianna. *Mobile Millinery Museum Collection.* $50-65.

A circlet of dried rose buds cap a long narrow veil. *Mobile Millinery Museum Collection.* $50-60.

Lacy wedding hat with shallow crown. *Mobile Millinery Museum Collection.* $80-100.

Peach roses form the foundation for a 1980s silk bouquet. $35-45.

A silk wedding bouquet c. 1985. *Mobile Millinery Museum Collection*. $35-45.

Bride Laura Russell in a gown designed in 1989.
The sleeve caps are inset with strands of beads.

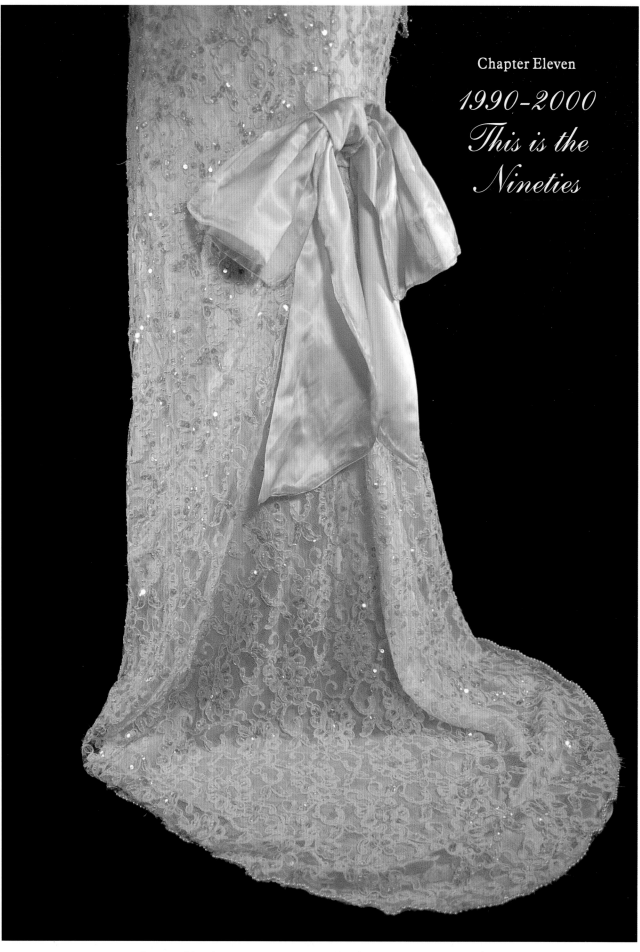

A mermaid train emerges under a satin bow, supported by a cone-shaped
length of stiffened tulle. *Mobile Millinery Museum Collection*. $600-800.

The nineties was a transitional decade for bridal design. Subtle changes to silhouette and fabrication occurred and ornamentation was taken to the extreme. One innovation was to create openings in the fabric and encircle them with lace and/or beading or fill them with transparent materials. Leg-of-mutton sleeves remained for a time but diminished in size.

Generous amounts of fabric went into the gowns at the outset of the decade but skirts tended to be circular rather than bell-shaped as before. Designers conceived countless methods of bustling chapel, cathedral, and circular trains. Snaps hid under embellishments, buttonholes were disguised in lace; even loop and pulley combinations were devised.

By 1995 a sleek sophisticated look was catching hold as young women looked to celebrity brides for inspiration. Bridal hats were given up altogether and veils might be worn with a bridal wreath of flowers, sequins, beads, or a combination of all three.

This beaded gown of polyester silk is completely washable. The train is supported by a heavy net underskirt and balances the weight of the heavily beaded bodice. *Mobile Millinery Museum Collection*. $500-600.

An enormous double bow dominates the back.

The stand-up collar can be folded down to reveal a bateau neckline.

Chapel length tulle veil gathered onto a hair band of sequins, beads, and faux pearls c. 1990. *Mobile Millinery Museum Collection*. $125-150.

Beading on center back bow is repeated on bodice and skirt.

Machine embroidered polyester chiffon overlay gown for a flower girl has attached crinoline and leg-of-mutton sleeves. Label: Angelina. *Mobile Millinery Museum Collection*. $75-100.

Dress and modesty jacket are appliquéd with machine lace, seed pearls and iridescent sequins. Jacket has self-fabric back button closure.

Back view of a sleeveless ivory gown of polyester satin. Attached, chapel train snaps together at each side, then loops over waist buttons to bustle the skirt for dancing. *Mobile Millinery Museum Collection.* $300-400.

This all-white garter in its original box is a nod to tradition in an age when brides are likely to wear pantyhose. *Mobile Millinery Museum Collection.* $20-25.

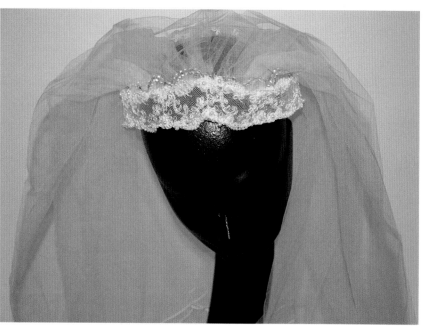

Fingertip veil and blusher of rayon tulle is set off by a crown of pearl dotted lace. *Mobile Millinery Museum Collection.* $150.

A crown of beads and sequins anchors a flyaway veil. *Courtesy of Mobile Millinery Museum Collection.* $250.

Silver cording and faux pearls wrap a bride's wired circle headpiece, adorned with polyester silk bow, roses, and lily-of-the-valley. *Mobile Millinery Museum Collection.* $60-75.

Side view showing sleeve detail.

Back view. Skirt is
bustled for dancing.

Bride Brigitte Grenier cried tears of joy when she found the dress of her dreams for her
wedding, August 28, 1998. The polyester-satin gown with attached cathedral train is heavily
beaded. Label: Mon Cherie Bridals Inc. *Courtesy of Brigitte Grenier*. $800-900.

Bride Tammy Burt in this wedding gown with enormous circle train. *Photo by Claude Stockley.*

Bridal cap, beaded to match gown supports a fingertip veil. *Mobile Millinery Museum Collection.* $100-150.

Skirt with attached cathedral train catches the light with inserts of beaded illusion.

Back view of skirt, bustled for dancing.

Tammy Burt's polyester satin gown with V-neck and back inserts of bridal illusion, wedding point sleeves and machine embroidery boasts seed pearls and iridescent sequins. Skirt with attached cathedral train catches the light with inserts of beaded illusion. Label: Alfred Angelo Inc. *Mobile Millinery Museum Collection.* $800-900.

A spray of silk flowers anchors a tulle veil. *Mobile Millinery Museum Collection.* $60-80.

A ruffle of tulle is set off by faux pearl beads on a wired crown. For a bridesmaid c. 1995. *Mobile Millinery Museum Collection*. $60-75.

A double flounce of vanilla chiffon mirrors a tiered overlay skirt. Bridal collar, five foot train. *Mobile Millinery Museum Collection*. $350-425.

Chapter Twelve
Brides of the New Millennium

Bride Corinne Watson September 15, 2001.

Corinne Watson took two years to plan her fairytale-themed wedding. She wanted every detail perfect, right down to the rhinestone magic wand carried by her flower girl. But when a family friend was murdered and her sister was diagnosed with a devastating illness, flowers, centerpieces, and bonbonieres seemed unimportant. Then, four days before her September 15th ceremony, terrorists attacked the world trade center. Watson added trailing black ribbons to her chiffon veil, out of respect for those brides whose wedding plans would never come to fruition.

Like Watson, many brides of the new millennium are opting for meaningful touches that personalize their look through embellishment and accessorization. The watchword so far is individualization. Gloves, hats, furs, and other forgotten accessories are enjoying a return to popularity as designers take a playful approach to their creations. Color is appearing in bridal wear designs and black is now seen on corset bodices and peek-a-boo crinolines.

With embellishments taken to the extreme in the 1990s, wedding gown designs of the new millennium are returning to clean, simple lines. A less-is-more approach has even been applied to bouquets, with brides now selecting small round or cascading arrangements of fresh flowers in ever-new color combinations.

With everything old truly new again, many contemporary brides have incorporated fashion elements of the past into their bridal look. The ball gown bodices of the fifties are now worn with stoles or fabric wraps, reminiscent of the glamorous thirties. Some brides are even taking a sentimental look at the gowns their mothers wore in the seventies and modernizing them by removing the sleeves and deepening the neckline.

Corinne Watson (nee Shephard) in a chiffon overlay gown. Bodice and upper sleeves are ornamented with crystal beads. Lower sleeves open at the elbow to produce an angel wing effect.

Chiffon overlay gown. Label: Pronovia. *Courtesy of Corinne Watson*. $600-800.

View showing angel wing sleeve and chiffon overlay skirt that separates in front.

Back view showing chiffon veil with trailing black ribbons.

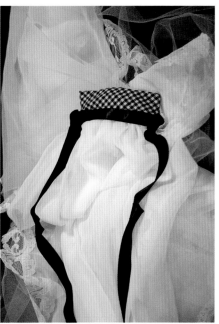

Bride Corinne Watson's beaded handbag, tiara, and "magic wand."

A similar gown with beaded bodice and chiffon sleeves. $500-600.

Silk tulle supports a chiffon veil on a headpiece of the bride's family tartan. *Courtesy of Corinne Watson*. $200-250.

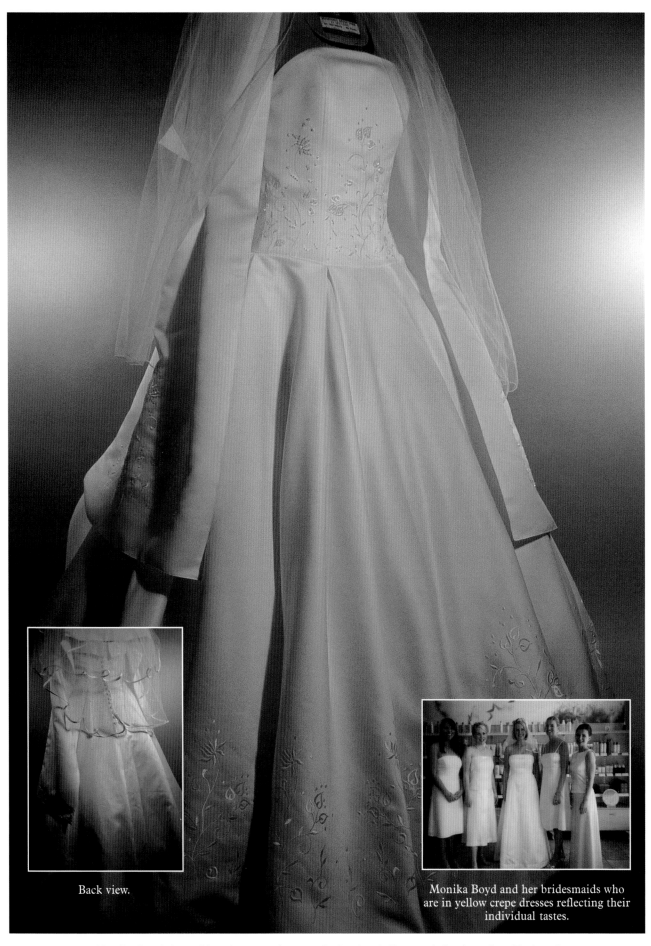

Back view.

Monika Boyd and her bridesmaids who
are in yellow crepe dresses reflecting their
individual tastes.

Monika Boyd chose this polyester satin gown for its simple lines and classic styling. Each end
of the self-fabric stole is weighted with beading to match the bodice and hem of the dress. A
two-tiered flyaway veil is edged in satin ribbon. *Courtesy of Monika Boyd.* $600-800.

October 2003: Meredith Baxter felt like Cinderella when she took her vows in a strapless gown and matching stole of polyester satin. Five layers of tulle crinoline support a box-pleated full skirt. Machine embroidered vine motif at the hem matches the crystal bead detail on bodice. *Courtesy of Meredith Maxwell.* $600-800.

Bride Meredith Maxwell chose to underlie her wedding gown with this red satin corset for a touch of the unexpected. Label: Frederick's of Hollywood. *Courtesy of Meredith Maxwell.* $50-60.

A rhinestone and faux pearl tiara anchors a flyaway veil. Ear rings and drop necklace coordinate nicely. *Courtesy of Meredith Maxwell.* $150-200.

Maid of honor Corinne Watson and bride Susan McCann in similarly styled spaghetti-strap gowns, 2003. Watson's ribbon-wrapped bouquet is reminiscent of a Victorian nosegay.

Corded satin purse and garter rests on a beaded wedding stole. 2003. *Courtesy of Meredith Maxwell.*

Headpiece, handbag, garter and hanky, all with petit point detail. *Courtesy of Larysa Kramer.* Ensemble: $250-350.

Close-up of floral headpiece.

Larysa Ilczyna's satin wedding gown with petit point embroidery was lovingly made by a relative. $800-1000.

Larysa Ilczyna designed her strapless satin wedding gown to be adorned with hand-stitched blue petit point at the neckline and hem to honor her Ukrainian heritage. She covered her arms with a fur stole for her walk down the aisle April 17, 2004. *Courtesy of Larysa Kramer.* $600-800.

Ribbon streamers with hand-stitched petit point trail from a silk flower headpiece. *Courtesy of Larysa Kramer.* $250-300.

Close up of handmade garter and bridal bag.

Hand embroidered bodice.

A bodice overlay of beaded illusion is a modest alternative to a strapless gown. Label: Venus. *Courtesy of Amberin Dookee.* $400-600.

Bride Lorraine Cutaia accessorized her wedding gown with platform sneakers for comfort, c. December 23, 2000.

Navy bows on hood and slashes punctuate a bride's cape of ribbon organza. *Courtesy of Corinne Watson.* $450-550.

French bride Isabelle Derler's elegant two-piece wedding suit with attached court train became a show stopper when she added a rose trimmed confection by Jean Paul Gauthier.

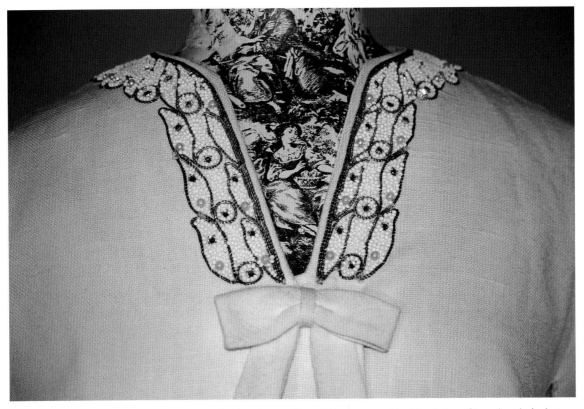

A contemporary bride chose to accessorize her ivory silk wedding gown with this vintage Chanel-style jacket, beaded about the neck with pearls and rhinestones. *Courtesy of Ardra Shephard.* $250.

Chapter Thirteen

The Life of a Collection

A bride-to-be searches the racks of a shop that specializes in remodeling vintage gowns.

Exhibiting a Vintage Gown

As we move further away from the twentieth century it becomes increasingly interesting to take a retrospective look at earlier trends in bridal fashion. For the past two seasons, the Prestige Bridal Show, Canada's longest running wedding showcase, has invited the Mobile Millinery Museum to include a selection of historic gowns in their fashion show extravaganza. Many contemporary brides and designers are looking to the past for inspiration.

Vintage wedding gowns are also making a second debut at silver and golden wedding anniversaries. Presented along with original wedding photos, these provide a focal point for guests and act as a sentimental touchstone for the former bride and groom.

Whether decorating for such an event, mounting a professional exhibit of historic wedding fashion, or undertaking to display a favorite piece decoratively in the home, careful consideration must be given to the manner in which a vintage gown will be supported. Placement considerations must also be addressed in order to protect an antique wedding gown from heat, strong light, and curious fingers. While it is a treat to see such treasures on display, properly cared for vintage textiles spend most of their lives in the dark, protected from extreme temperatures, moisture, and air contaminants.

Care and Preservation of Vintage Wedding Gowns

All efforts should be made to prevent hanging vintage garments on hangers as this places stress on delicate fibers. Ideally, wedding gowns should be stored flat in archival boxes with acid-free tissue paper slipped between the fabric folds. Vintage textiles can also be safely stored in shallow drawers designed for this purpose. The American National Standards Institute and the Canadian Conservation Institute set out temperature and humidity guidelines for textile storage to guard against pollutants, moisture and/or excessive dryness.

Making it Fit

The dress forms and mannequins available today are not always a suitable fit for the undersized wedding costumes of yesteryear. Early garments are often too small for even the tiniest of these. Some Victorian girls married as young teens and had corseted waistlines to match their age and wedding gowns of the Second World War are also tiny. The women who wore them became lean due to the rationing of sugar, butter, and gasoline. Museum curators have become creative in their approach to displaying such pieces, using everything from chicken wire and papier machier, to panty hose and quilt batting, as the building blocks for custom mannequins.

The Costume Museum of Canada has used various mannequin-building techniques over the years and currently creates life-sized, naturally posed body doubles, similar in appearance to cabbage patch dolls. Collections Coordinator, Brenda Hamer, describes the process:

"The mannequins that are more recent are made using polyethylene foam sheets for the torso. The garment is first measured and the measurements are then transferred to the polyethylene, keeping in mind the shape of the human body. Before the disks can be glued together, flat surfaces of the polyethylene foam must be covered with polyethylene plastic or vapor barrier. This provides a non-porous surface for the glue. The disk shapes are then cut out of the foam and hot-glued and layered horizontally upward to form a torso. The torso would then be carved to fit the desired shape. It is a good idea to check the mannequin periodically for fit by placing a large t-shirt over it and then trying on the historic garment. When the mannequin form has reached the desired shape, it can be wrapped and padded out in polyester batting. The batting can then be sewn with large basting stitches. A pre-washed cotton or four-way stretch fabric can be used to cover the body. It is best to hide the seams where they will not be visible."

Behind the Seams at a Vintage Wedding Gown Exhibit

In 1999, a group of more than thirty women gathered at Prince Edward Island's Rod Mill River Resort to pay tribute to eighty-seven year old former seamstress, Bessie Dumville, the woman who designed and crafted their wedding gowns over a period of forty years. Many of the designer's creations were displayed at the event.

In October of 2001, Bessie's achievement was celebrated once again when forty-six of Bessie's former brides went to their closets and trunks to retrieve their cherished dresses for a unique textile exhibit at Summerside, P.E.I., entitled *The Bridal Creations Of Bessie Dumville*. The exhibit "looked like a room full of angels," said vintage clothing enthusiast Donna Young.

If the dresses could talk one might reveal how a former client presented Bessie with a linen tablecloth the day before the wedding, requesting that she use it to fashion a jacket. Another might tell of the catalogue and magazine photos Bessie utilized in order to understand the vision of her clients. And after the wedding? Dumville remembers the maiden and married names of all her former clients and takes pride in the fact that only one of her "girls" subsequently divorced.

Searching for Vintage Wedding Attire

It is wise to take into consideration the condition, label (if any), age, and workmanship of a garment as well as its charm and potential before deciding upon a purchase. If the gown is to be worn, fit will also become a factor. Turn the garment inside out to examine its construction. Look for generous seam allowances or opportunities to insert panels.

A large water stain.

Damage and Deterioration

Very early wedding gowns may show general signs of wear and tear as they were worn on several occasions whereas one-time-only gowns might reveal injury from being worn outdoors, danced in, or inadequately cleaned and stored. Look for the following damage or deterioration on aged wedding gowns:

~ Rust spots, caused by flowers.
~ Shredding of weighted silks.
~ Perspiration stains on early rayon silks.
~ Yellowing of natural fabrics.
~ Greyish hue to aged synthetic fabrics.
~ Missing buttons on mid-twentieth century pieces.
~ Torn tulle on 1950s gowns.
~ Burn holes on synthetic fabrics.
~ Loss of beads.
~ Torn and soiled hems.

Documenting a Vintage Wedding Gown Collection

Whether you are preserving for posterity the dress, shoes, and bouquet from your own wedding, taking care of the family weddings repository, or have become a serious hoarder of vintage bridal fashion, knowing and documenting what you have will enhance the historic and financial value of your assortment.

Begin by collecting as much information as you can about each acquisition including age, fabrication, style, original owner, designer, value, etc. Record the information in an organized fashion on index cards or in a loose-leaf binder. Allow space for a photo or sketch and record the item's location.

A group of three or more objects linked by theme, origin, or purpose constitutes a collection. A collection built around a bridal costume theme need not limit itself solely to wedding gowns and accessories but might expand to include bride dolls, cake toppers, wedding invitations, photos, or any item depicting a bride in period costume.

These bride dolls in 1960s garb are an easy to store alternative to the real thing.

Collecting Victorian and Edwardian Wedding Portrait Photos

As part of a recent costume exhibit at Toronto's Royal Ontario Museum, a series of photographs stood in for a wedding gown of weighted silk which was too fragile to exhibit and certain to deteriorate if handled. In a similar spirit of practicality, many vintage bridal costume enthusiasts are turning to Victorian and Edwardian wedding portrait photos as an alternative to the costly and hard to find wedding gowns, veils, hats, and parasols of that period. Other collectors are using late 19th and early 20th century photos (1860-1920) to enhance an existing costume collection or to inspire reproduction designs.

Less expensive, more durable, and easier to store than many of the delicate vintage costumes they depict, period portrait photos provide an accurate record of Victorian and Edwardian fashion and can form an exciting collection unto themselves.

Apache Wedding Blessing

Now you will feel no rain
For each of you will be shelter to the other.
Now each of you will feel no cold
For each of you will be warmth to the other.
Now there is no loneliness for you
For each of you will be companion to the other.
Now you are two persons
But there is one life before you.
Go now to your dwelling place to enter into the days of your togetherness
And may your days be good and long upon the earth.

Glossary

Astrakhan: A long curly fur from the astrakhan lamb.
Balayeuse: A removable dust ruffle sewn to the underside of a hem.
Blusher : A length of veiling that covers the face.
Broderie Anglaise: An embroidery technique worked in white cotton which uses white thread to outline open areas of the fabric.
Bubble toque: A high-crowned, brimless hat of the 1960s designed to cover a bouffant hairstyle.
Bustle: A back extension placed below the waist of a skirt.
Cartwheel: A shallow crowned, wide brim hat.
Chemisette: A Victorian and Edwardian ladies undergarment of muslin, linen, lawn, mull, lace, silk, or embroidery, which covers the arms and décolletage.
Cloche: A bell-shaped close-fitting hat introduced in the 1920s.
Cochineal: A natural red dye made from boiling the cochineal beetle.
Corsage: Refers to bodice, fabric draped over the ribcage portion of a woman's dress, or flowers used to decorate a costume.
Crin: A lacy straw made from horsehair.
Cutwork: Eyelet embroidery.
Crewel: A tapestry of embroidered yarn.
Crystalette: A synthetic fabric with a metallic sheen.
Damask: A rich looking fabric made in the jacquard loom with fancy weaves and embellishments.
Duchesse: A soft, high luster satin, tightly woven.
Empiecement: A yoke-like insert at the neck of a bodice.
Faille: A lightweight ribbed silk.
Flapper: A term used to describe young women of the twenties who defied social convention.
Grosgrain: Corded or ribbed silk ribbon.
Guipure lace: A heavy lace of individual patterns joined by connecting threads.
Indigo: A blue dye made from a root powder.

Jacquard: A patterned weave worked on a loom.
Lisse: A transparent, tissue-like silk.
Mousseline de soie: A silk muslin with the appearance of gauze.
Muslin: Cotton fabric with a transparent quality.
Organdie: A stiffened cotton with a translucent quality.
Pamela: A wide-brim hat with close-fitting crown.
Pannier: A style emphasizing the hips as if a pair of baskets were carried on either side.
Pashmina: A cashmere shawl woven from the wool of Himalayan mountain goats.
Penoir: A see-through nightgown often with a matching robe.
Petticoat: A slip-like undergarment favored by Victorians. Usually of cotton or silk and falling from the waist or shoulders.
Picot: Ornamental edging of small loops done by hand or machine.
Postillions: Long, frontal bodice extensions to a jacket or vest.
Princess Style: A one-piece fitted style often pleated from bust to hips with no waist seam.
Raglan: A sleeve that extends to the neck.
Rayon: A manufactured fabric from regenerated cellulose fiber.
Ruched: Tightly gathered.
Sans Culottes: French for "without pants".
Satin: A fabric with a smooth, lustrous surface. Made from silk, acetate, or rayon, it enjoys a wide variation of weights.
Smocked: Embellished with rows of gathered stitches.
Strass: Cut steel.
Taffeta: A stiff lustrous fabric.
Train: A trailing skirt.
Twill: A woven fabric with parallel ridges.
Visite: A short wrap designed to emphasize the bustle.
Watteau train: A train that falls from the shoulder blades to the hem of a gown or beyond.

Bibliography

Akiko Fukai. *Fashion, A History from the 18ᵗʰ to the 20ᵗʰ Century, The Collection of the Kyoto Costume Institute.* London, New York, Paris etc.: Taschen, 2002.

Ball, Joanne Dubbs and Torem-Craig, Caroline. *Wedding Traditions, Here Comes The Bride.* Dubuque, Iowa: Antique Trader Books, 1997.

Bardey, Catherine. *Wearing Vintage.* New York, New York: Black Dog & Leventhal Publishers, Inc., 2002.

Berman, Ann E. *Vintage Style.* New York, New York: Harper Collins, 2000.

Blum, Stella. *Victorian Fashions & Costumes from Harper's Bazaar: 1867 – 1898.* New York, New York: Dover Publications Inc., 1974.

Chase, Deborah. *Terms of Adornment.* New York, New York: Harper Collins, 1999.

Dolan, Maryanne. *Vintage Clothing, 1880 – 1960.* Florence, Alabama: Books America, 1987.

Dubin, Tiffany and Berman, Ann E. *Vintage Style.* New York, New York: Harper Collins Publishers. 2000.

Eaton, Nancy. *Your Vintage Wedding.* New York, New York: HarperCollins Publishers, 2001.

Fraser, Sylvia. *A Woman's Place.* Toronto, Ontario: Key Porter Books Ltd., 1997.

Frost, Patricia. *Miller's Collecting Textiles.* Great Britain: Octopus Publishing Group Ltd., 2000.

Hansen, Henny Harald. *Costume Cavalcade.* Copenhagen, Denmark: Politikens Forlag, 1954.

Harris, Carol. *Miller's Collecting Fashion & Accessories.* London, England: Octopus Publishing Group Ltd., 2000.

Hemingway, Karen. *The Essential Guide to Embroidery.* London, England: Murdoch Books Ltd., 2002.

Hillyer-Shephard, Norma. *Dear Harry: The Firsthand Account of a World War I Infantryman.* Burlington, Ontario: Brigham Press, 2003.

Langley, Susan. *Vintage Hats & Bonnets.* Paducah, Kentucky: Collector Books. 1998.

Lansdell, Avril. *Wedding Fashions, 1860 – 1980.* Buckinghamshire, U.K.: Shire Publications, 1997.

Lipsett, Otto, Linda. *To Love & To Cherish: Brides Remembered.* Lincolnwood, Illinois: The Quilt Digest Press, 1997.

Malaher, Rosemary. *Dugald Costume Museum The Story.* Dugald, Manitoba. 1989.

McDowell, Colin. *Hats Status, Style and Glamour.* London, England: Thames and Hudson Ltd. 1992.

Milbank, Caroline, Rennolds. *The Couture Accessory.* New York: Harry N. Abrams, Inc. Publishers. 2002.

Mulvey, Kate and Richards, Melissa. *Decades of Beauty.* New York, New York: Reed Consumer Books Limited, 1998.

Nebens, Amy M. *Traditional Gowns.* New York, New York: Sterling Publishing Company, Inc.

Palmer, Alexandra. *Couture & Commerce.* Toronto, Ontario: UBC Press, 2001.

Reilly, Maureen and Mary Beth Detrich. *Women's Hats of the 20ᵗʰ Century.* Atglen, Pennsylvania: Schiffer Publishing Ltd., 1997.

Severn, Bill. *Here's Your Hat.* New York: David McKay Company Inc., 1963.

Smith, Desire. *Hats with Values.* West Chester, Pennsylvania: Schiffer Publishing Ltd., 1996.

Wilcox, Claire. *A Century of Bags: Icons of Style in the 20th Century.* London, England: Quarto Publishing. 1998.

Wilcox, Turner. *The Mode In Hats And Headdress.* United States: Scribners, 1945.

What's What 1902. London, England, 1902.

Index

Alfred Angelo, 179, 200
Algo, 174
Angelina, 196
Apron, wedding, 24, 62, 140
Austin, 138
Avida Boutique, 182
Bessie Dumville, 211
Blouse, wedding, 11, 47, 50, 53, 54, 55
Blue Bird Dress, Toronto, 189
Boa, 10
Bolero, 82, 83, 129,131
Borden's Ladies Wear, 102
Bouquets, 8, 16, 22, 24, 54, 63, 64, 76, 79, 131, 164, 165, 180, 183, 185, 186, 187, 193, 200, 202, 205
Bourne & Hollingsworth, 11, 69
Boyer Exclusive Models, Lachine, 91
Buckle, 73, 79, 83, 104
Bustle, 6, 28, 29, 34, 80, 195, 197, 199, 200
Camisole, 37, 38, 62
Capelet, 14, 31, 130
Caplan's, 93
Casa Loma, 4, 5, 13
Chemisette, 40, 41, 53, 54, 56
Coat, wedding, 81, 103, 117, 118, 125, 127, 132
Collar, bateau, 195
    bridal, 40, 44, 45, 49, 54, 166, 201
    detachable, 33
    rolled, 115
    ruffled, 172
    sailor, 50, 53
    scalloped, 66
    shawl, 60
    stand-up, 109, 110, 111, 129, 151, 195
    "V", 55
Coronet, 101, 103
Corset, 16, 28, 40, 44, 92, 117, 118, 205
Costume Museum of Canada, 211
Crinoline, 16, 17, 22, 32, 117, 119, 125, 127, 129, 147, 205
Cummerbund, 36, 40, 43, 46, 49, 56, 125
David E. Rae, 154, 182
Dentelles, 132
Dolls, 7, 20, 212
Dress, best, 24, 55
    bridesmaid's, 12, 40, 44, 46, 87, 110, 143, 151, 163, 175, 177, 204
        Christening, 20
        Delphos, 51
        going-away, 24, 40, 115, 150, 161
        second day, 24, 29, 30
Dust ruffle, 43, 56, 163, 166, 172, 177
Edward VII, 26
Eaton's, 61, 99, 112, 140
Epaulettes, 53, 105
Fan, 170
Flapper, 8, 10, 63, 64, 66, 70, 71, 72, 73, 76, 78
Frederick's of Hollywood, 205
Garter, 116, 149, 198, 205, 206, 207
Glover, Fry & Co., 28
Gloves, 17, 18, 24, 32, 40, 41, 53, 56, 90, 91, 92, 102, 116, 118, 137, 138, 159, 183
Goodwin's Ladies Wear, 53
Handbags, 17, 32, 37, 75, 91, 137, 158, 159, 162, 183, 203, 205, 206, 207
Hankie, bridal, 24, 25, 42, 44, 45, 132, 138, 206
Harper's Bazaar, 64
Hem, handkerchief, 63, 70, 78, 183
    petal-point, 60
    scalloped, 184

Hood, 14, 77, 184, 208
House of Nu-Mode, 176
Ideal Maid, 90
Irene of Montreal, 161
Jean Paul Gautier, 209
Jo-Anne, 129
Juliet cap, 12, 13, 58, 65, 91, 98, 111, 131, 132, 192
Jumpsuit, 6, 182
Kleinert's Dress Shields, 28
Lady Elizabeth Bowes-Lyon, 64
Lord and Taylor, 119
Lucyane, 159
Mary Janes, 92
Mary, Queen of Scots, 101
Merry widow, 127
Miriam Originals, 86
Mobile Millinery Museum, 4,13, 210
Molyneux, 64
Mon Cherie Bridals Inc., 199
Musee Mississquoi, 4
Necklines, bateau, 195
    Bertha, 92
    cowl, 77
    high, 22, 45, 56
    hooded, 77
    illusion, 17, 92, 107, 116, 119, 132, 166, 191
    scalloped, 122
    scoop, 90
    sweetheart, 87, 92, 102, 103, 127
    "U", 112
    "V", 66, 82, 84, 121, 125, 164, 182, 188, 191, 200
Parasols, 6, 39, 47, 48, 164
Paris Gloves, 138
Parlour Clothing Co., 174
Party Time Fashions Ltd., 182
Peplum, 12, 33, 92, 108, 115
Perfect Junior Formal Ltd., 127, 147
Petticoats, 22, 30, 36, 46, 58, 62
Philip Warde, 154
Prestige Bridal Show, 210
Princess Alice, 22
Princess Mary, 64
Princess Vicky, 22
Pronovia, 203
Queen Victoria, 22
Royal Ontario Museum, 213
Ruthe Original, 114
Schiaparelli, 159
Sears, 147
Shamish & Yofi, 166
Silhouette, A-line, 129, 139, 140, 144, 148, 163
    ballerina, 118, 121, 123, 126, 131
    ballgown, 97, 106, 117, 118, 127, 130, 132, 202
    bias-cut, 77, 82, 88, 114
    empire, 90, 130, 139, 146, 151, 152, 163, 167, 179
    pannier, 14, 111, 122
    pigeon-breasted, 52
    princess, 40, 100, 101, 129
    pumpkin, 14, 118, 139
    shapeless, 63, 71, 72, 76, 78, 81
    sheath, 14, 139, 160
Simpson's, 103
Skirt, bell, 132, 133, 195
    circle, 86, 195
    gored, 84
    hobble, 54, 56, 58, 59
    pumpkin, 14, 118, 139
    short, 64, 94, 142, 143, 150
    straight-cut, 13

wedding, 35, 46, 47, 48, 53
Sleeves, angel-wing, 202, 203
    bell, 163
    Camelot, 163
    cap, 84, 116, 123
    detachable, 8
    dolman, 118, 129
    double, 60, 61, 188
    drop, 58, 59
    leg-of-mutton, 195,196
    off-the-shoulder, 17, 119
    pelican, 79
    raglan, 81
    short, 118, 146, 168, 174
    three-quarter, 40, 41, 46, 49, 52, 54, 62
    transparent, 180
    wedding point, 10, 12, 65, 85, 101, 112, 121, 129, 132, 152, 200
Slippers, 94, 102
Stole, 8, 9, 79, 204, 205, 207
Suit, wedding, 53, 54, 92, 95, 105, 108, 119, 209
Train, bridal, 13, 14, 22
    cathedral, 14, 113, 118, 195, 199, 200
    chapel, 9, 12, 14, 28, 85, 117, 152, 167, 169, 190, 195, 197
    circular, 118, 184, 195, 200
    court, 14, 182, 209
    detachable, 8, 14, 28, 139, 169, 181
    fan-tail, 115
    mermaid, 194
    pannier, 14
    Royal, 14
    split, 23, 120
    sweep, 14, 29, 36, 46, 56, 65
    triangular, 88
    Watteau, 14, 146, 149, 160
Trousseau, 24, 38, 52, 138, 153
Undergarments, 16, 17, 22, 37, 38, 44, 45, 46, 64, 88, 89, 90, 139
Veils, blusher 16, 157, 164, 165, 180
    cathedral, 16
    chapel, 16, 120, 182, 196
    chiffon, 16
    court, 16,
    circular, 157,
    embroidered, 100
    fingertip, 16, 97, 171, 173, 185, 186
    flyaway, 16, 132, 134, 136, 155,157, 181, 198, 204, 205
    lace, 16, 68
    mantilla, 16, 68, 74
    Royal, 16
    split, 23, 36
Venus, 208
Visite, 22, 29
Waist, belted, 71, 79, 81, 83, 104, 128, 184
    dropped, 63, 64, 67
    pouched, 40, 50
    princess, 86
    scalloped, 119
Wedding chest, 46
Weighted silk, 36, 212
Wraps, 22, 26, 77, 202
Wreaths, 15, 195
Yoke, 14, 29, 36, 44, 49, 107, 120, 130, 132, 145, 160,172, 182, 184